The Mystery of
The Iceman

The Mystery of
The Iceman

Exploring one of the greatest
archaeological mysteries of all time

OLIVER THOMAS & KENDA MCHALE
Artwork by O. Thomas

WESTBOW
PRESS
A DIVISION OF THOMAS NELSON

WestBow Press books may be ordered through booksellers or by contacting:

WestBow Press
A Division of Thomas Nelson
1663 Liberty Drive
Bloomington, IN 47403
www.westbowpress.com
1-(866) 928-1240

Unless otherwise noted, all Scripture passages are taken
from the King James Version of the Bible.

ISBN: 978-1-4497-9559-7 (sc)
ISBN: 978-1-4497-9560-3 (hc)
ISBN: 978-1-4497-9558-0 (e)

Library of Congress Control Number: 2013909002

Printed in the United States of America.

WestBow Press rev. date: 07/02/2013

"When you have eliminated the impossible, whatever remains, however improbable, must be the truth."

—Sherlock Holmes, *The Sign of the Four*

INTRODUCTION

Let me begin by informing the reader that when you see the pronoun *I* used in this book, it really means *we,* because this book was researched and written by a father-and-daughter team. For simplicity's sake we have chosen to pen the book as one author. Being a minister, I have devoted myself to the nurture of my church, but whenever I have the opportunity, I delve into my other true love, the study of ancient biblical history. In the course of my delving, I became fascinated with an extremely old, frozen body found in the Austro-Italian Alps known to the world as the Iceman.

I remember the first radio news report in September 1991 briefly describing how a fully intact human body had been found in Europe that might be more than 3,000 years old. Eventually when the 5,300-year-old age of the Iceman became evident, he was a lead story in newspapers around the world. He certainly created quite a hubbub in Austria, where scientists and reporters almost became a mob trying to get a look or take a picture. All the excitement caused by this mummy piqued my interest, so I was sure to read any new information coming out. Almost immediately I realized that from the standpoint of biblical history, this man probably lived during the time period of the first ten generations of men listed in the Bible.

Time passed, and the Iceman's novelty faded. Nevertheless, every new discovery about the mummy would still make the front page and generate a slew of scientific journal articles. During this time another odd story began to develop. With the death of Helmut Simon, the man who found the Iceman's body, rumors of a curse began to circulate. Simon was the fourth to die of the four people involved with the discovery and removal of the Iceman from the mountain glacier. It wasn't until the death of the seventh person directly involved in the discovery of the Iceman that I took notice. With the death of Dr. Tom Loy in 2005, I began to research the Iceman in earnest. This book is the culmination of a fifteen-year study.

I have examined a number of diverse features unique to the Iceman that demonstrate this mummy may be far more important than anyone has realized. In my opinion, the Iceman is nothing less than a human time capsule preserving evidence of a monumental tragedy at the very dawn of recorded history.

I shared with my daughter some of the interesting research coming from Europe about this Stone Age man. We became more and more interested in the Iceman not only because of his extreme age but also the uniqueness of his preservation. At this point my daughter began to do her own research, finding many additional intriguing facts from scientific journals. She also began to document and write down each discovery, which is how this book started to take form.

From the era in which the Iceman lived we have little evidence of archaeological value. We find many rudimentary tools, rock carvings, and the remnants of dwellings, but other than these items, which have deteriorated, we have very little to go on. Then out of this void we discover a fully preserved human with his tools, clothing, and DNA intact. Like a phantom, the Iceman emerges from the fog of time. In view of the information we can glean from his discovery, the Iceman is one of the greatest artifacts ever found. But to interpret the information, we must put him in his proper historical setting.

Our objective in presenting this book is to take the reader on a journey—actually an expedition into a lost world. Taking the evidence found on the Iceman, we will reconstruct the past in the most astounding fashion. This book is a study in ancient history, arranging people and events according to records passed down through the centuries. This book is a theological dissertation, addressing human motives both good and evil, while attempting to expose the spiritual condition of men and mankind as a whole. It ventures into ancient prophecies and future revelations. Looking as far back as possible, we use the oldest written language as a source for interpreting future events. This book is a scientific research hypothesis examining various aspects of archaeology, genetics, and microbiology. It is a mystery novel, a tale of betrayal, murder, intrigue, and curses.

Before I finish, I would like to say this as a proud father: this book is a great accomplishment in both the literary sense and in analytical thinking. My daughter has skillfully engineered all its differing aspects into an exciting, fast-moving narrative that you may find hard to put down. The book envelops all these various subjects at the same time so the reader will not be overwhelmed with sterile facts or scientific jargon. She has also gone to great lengths to maintain the integrity of the work with thorough research of all the material used in the overall concept as well as each specific subject. I would like her to know how much I appreciate and love her, and how incredibly fortunate I feel to have such an amazing coauthor.

In summation, we hope you enjoy learning about the remarkable discovery presented here, and that you are enriched by the knowledge it brings. People from every walk of life can benefit from the experiences of our common ancestors, regardless of their secular or religious outlook. This will be a small investment of your time, but you could realize a great harvest of wisdom. Age to age it has proved true that those who do not learn the lessons of history are doomed to repeat it. With that final thought may I suggest that you find a warm, quiet, comfortable place; relax; and clear your mind. A hot cup of tea or coffee might be nice. Now let's not just read a book ...Let's go exploring.

This book is dedicated to Abel, the son of Adam: a man of the Spirit, as his name implies, and a young shepherd who pleased God. Though his life was short, his legacy has endured for thousands of years. May we always give the Lord our best—like the noble heart of Abel.

Also for my dear friend Marie Bartholomew, who recently went to be with the Lord. Thank you for your encouragement to write this book. Marie, we miss you so much!

Contents

Introduction. ix

Chapter 1 The Miraculous Iceman 1

Chapter 2 Raising Cain. 10

Chapter 3 The Way of Cain. 18

Chapter 4 The Markings 26

Chapter 5 Geographical Locations. 35

Chapter 6 5,000-Year-Old Murder Mystery Solved? . . . 47

Chapter 7 Antediluvian DNA 67

Chapter 8 The Curse 78

Chapter 9 The Sign 96

Chapter 10 The Verdict 107

Chapter 11 Are You Abel? 120

Addendum: Ancient Historical Records of Cain 129

Bibliography. .145

LIST OF ILLUSTRATIONS

1. The Iceman in the Primeval Forest - Title Page

2. Feet of the Iceman - Page 3

3. Northern Italy Discovery Site of Otzi - Page 5

4. Putting a Face on the Legend of Cain - Page 12

5. Iceman on Display in His Vault - Page 17

6. The First Murder – Page 19

7. The Weathered Face of the Iceman – Page 21

8. Placement of Markings on the Iceman – Page 28

9. Illustration of Tav X Tattoos Found on Otzi – Page 29

10. Illustration of Vav I Tattoos Found on Otzi – Page 30

11. Illustration of the Iceman's Wrist Tattoo – Page 33

12. Ancient Alphabet – Page 34

13. Castle Juval – Page 43

14. Map of Ancient Stone Age Village Juval – Page 43

15. Iceman Killed by Arrowhead Made by His Own Clan
    – Page 52

16. Neolithic Agriculture Tools Compared with Otzi's Ax
    – Page 57

17. The Iceman Puts Moss in His Wounds – Page 58

18. Death of the Iceman – Page 66

19. The Deluge – Page 69

20. Woolly Mammoth Frozen While Still Standing – Page 71

21. Drawing of the Oxyrhynchus Papyri, or P-115 – Page 103

22. XIC Found in the Ancient Alphabet – Page 104

23. Example of Iceman's Teeth, Showing Extreme Bruxism
    – Page 109

24. Example of Neolithic Petroglyph Showing X-Man
    – Page 114

25. Cain the Hunter and Wanderer – Page 117

26. Cain in the Land of Nod – Page 155

Chapter 1

The Miraculous Iceman

THE MYSTERY OF the Iceman begins on the Day of Atonement September 19, 1991. On the Hebrew calendar this is the tenth day of Tishri, also called Yom Kippur. It is the most important day of the year for those of the Jewish faith.

On Yom Kippur, Jewish tradition requires people to reflect on the story of Cain and Abel. Many Jews believe this was the day, several thousand years ago, that Abel made an atoning sacrifice to God and earned his favor. At the same time, Cain gave an offering that disappointed God. Cain became so jealous of his brother that he killed him and buried his body.

On the Day of Atonement, during the course of the remembrance, questions are asked as reflections. One question the rabbi asks is, "Where is your brother?"—the same question

God asked Cain. This question will lead us through a fascinating journey into the dawn of history.

September 19, 1991, was also a significant date in modern archaeology. This was the day an astonishing discovery was made, a discovery that would change the world's view of history. In the upper region of a melting Alpine glacier, a man's body was found protruding from a frozen pond. Initially, it was thought to be the remains of an unfortunate hiker, but it turned out to be the oldest, fully preserved human mummy ever found. After closer examination, the frozen corpse proved to be that of a man who lived more than 5,000 years ago. He was discovered by hikers who were exploring the Otz Valley of the Italian Alps near the border of Austria and soon after was nicknamed "Otzi the Iceman."

Today, this body is kept in its own museum at Bolzano, Italy, in a specially designed refrigerated vault (South Tyrol Museum of Archaeology, 2011). Scientists from around the world study the body, and their new discoveries become headline news in scientific journals and on the internet. However, there is more to the Iceman than meets the eye, even more than the scientific eyes of X-rays, CT scans, and electron microscopes.

Advanced scientific equipment has opened a window into the past, unearthing a mystery worthy of a Sir Arthur Conan Doyle novel. With all we have learned about the Iceman, we have come to a point where we can evaluate the evidence and draw conclusions about some fundamental, yet unanswered, questions. With an emphasis on logic, this study will lead to an astounding conclusion. As a guiding principle, we will use

Sherlock Holmes's famous motto, "It's elementary, Watson, the simplest explanation is usually the correct one," adding this caveat: in God's economy nothing happens by accident.

This crucial fact must not be overlooked: the very existence of a human body that's approximately 5,300 years old and in a highly preserved condition is probably the result of supernatural intervention. This is not an exaggeration if we carefully weigh the evidence. To get some perspective on just how old the Iceman is, consider the following facts: the Great Pyramid of Giza, in Egypt, is the only remaining wonder of the famous Seven Wonders of the Ancient World, even though it is far older than the other six; in fact, it was already ancient when the others were being built. The other great structures have weathered, eroded, and crumbled into dust. The only reason the pyramid still stands is its amazing design of solid-rock construction and sloped sides that defy gravity.

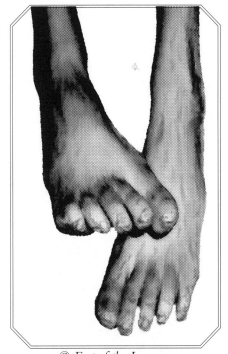

A general consensus among archaeologists places construction of the Great Pyramid around 2300 BC. Carbon dating of the Iceman indicates he lived about 3300 BC. *Miraculous* is the word we should use when we look at the feet of a man who

© *Feet of the Iceman.*
Artwork by O. Thomas

walked the earth a thousand years before the Great Pyramid was built.

So how did the Iceman's body remain intact for an astounding 5,300 years? There are two distinct reasons why this corpse was so well preserved. The first is that it was covered in ice shortly after the man died, so only minimal deterioration occurred. Experts who have examined the body when it was thawed say it still looks fresh (*Death of the Iceman, 2002*).

Unlike other mummies that have brittle, dry skin and powdery bones that crumble when touched, this body is intact with flesh, bone, and muscles. The eyes, brain, and tongue still remain in the skull. The heart, liver, and lungs remain in his chest (Spindler, 1996).

This body was not just dehydrated or frozen; it actually was freeze-dried by extremely cold wind that removed most of the water from it. According to an article in the *Journal of Archaeological Science*, Otzi is the world's most famous freeze-dried mummy and is an extraordinarily rare find. The article says, "Among natural mummies, those produced through freeze-drying are by far the best as they unite the preservation of the anatomical and cellular structures to that of many biological molecules. Unfortunately, freeze-desiccated mummies are relatively rare" (Rollo et al., 2007). To this I would like to add the fact that Otzi is far older than any other freeze-dried mummy ever found. Ice mummies are found primarily in the Andes Mountains of South America, and few are more than a thousand years old.

Scientists attribute the excellent state of Otzi's body to the freeze-drying process (Ermini, 2008). The fact that the water was removed saved him from the destruction caused by the freezing of wet tissue. Normally, frozen cells rupture and deteriorate quickly. After the body was freeze-dried, it was encased in ice and hidden away for more than fifty centuries.

© *Northern Italy Discovery Site of Otzi.* Artwork by O. Thomas

The second reason the body is so well preserved is the propitious location where the Iceman fell to his death. He collapsed into a small trench when he succumbed to wounds to be described later. It was in this trench that the icy, cold, dry wind blasted away the moisture from his body. This dehydration process lasted for approximately three or four weeks before it began snowing. It continued to snow until a massive glacier, estimated to have been as much as 200 feet thick, formed over the body.

It just so happened that this trench lay crosswise to the glacier's movement, preventing it from sliding along with the ice's slow movement (South Tyrol Museum of Archaeology). This immobilized the body, keeping it in the exact position where it fell. Had his body not fallen into this protective depression, the Iceman wouldn't exist today. He would have been ground to bits through the ages (Hall, 2007).

These fortuitous conditions are remarkable to say the least. What are the odds that a person would die while falling into a protective trench and then become completely freeze-dried just in time for the start of an ice age? What are the odds that the body would stay totally frozen for more than five thousand years? This is an archaeological dream come true!

Why did the Iceman suddenly appear? Most people refer to it as pure luck. In 1991, a huge dust storm blew across Europe from the Sahara Desert (Kutschera, n.d.). The dust covered the Alps and made the mountains dark, causing the absorption of more sunlight than normal. Along with an unusually hot summer, the ice melted enough so that the body was exposed for the first time. As was realized the next spring, this rapid melting of ice lasted only a short time, because the winter snowfall buried the discovery site with twenty feet of fresh snow. Who would find this body in such a desolate area?

History was changed when two hikers decided to take an unfamiliar path and walked right up to a human body protruding from the ice. They went back to a lodge and reported it to local officials. The policeman who came to retrieve the body could have destroyed it. He drilled into the Iceman's hip and tore apart the cloak, trying to extricate the body. Fortunately, the drill he was using ran out of power before more damage was done. Officials had to wait another week to recover the body with a pickax (Fowler, 2000).

Had the ice kept melting for weeks or even days longer, the body would have decomposed rapidly into a pile of bones. These critical circumstances came about with perfect timing and sequence. I suppose we could say this situation might happen about once every 6,000 years. Or could this be the hand of God preserving this person's body for a future age and revealing it at a specific time for a higher purpose?

Since the body's discovery more than two decades ago, scientists have examined the Iceman intensely. He has been subjected to numerous state-of-the-art scientific tests. The results have been nothing less than astounding. Had the Iceman been discovered seventy-five or a hundred years earlier, the body would have been given a proper burial and forgotten. Even fifty years earlier, mankind would not have had the technology to determine how old he was, his last meal, the cause of death, his DNA, or even minute details such as the bacterium and other matter found in his intestines.

The ice encasement, however, melted away at the right time in human history when knowledge had advanced far beyond the realms of what would have been imagined even a generation ago. There is much to be learned from this body that relates directly to our present age, which leads us to the purpose of this study.

The intent here is to pose an answer to the mystery arising from the finding of Otzi. The scientific world is struggling to find out who this man is. I don't believe Otzi is merely an enigma or a freak of nature; we can read his body like a book. I see Otzi as a translator of archaeology who joins biblical history to modern science. Otzi is like the touchstone that causes the ancient and modern worlds to collide. Can the modern world now answer these specific questions about a man who lived at the dawn of history? Questions to be examined in this study include the following: Who was this man? From where did he come? Who murdered him and why? Was he a cold-blooded killer? Is there really a curse attached to him?

As more details came to light about the Iceman's age and how he died, a ghostly figure from the ancient past began to emerge. He is a figure who bears remarkable similarities to Otzi. This person lived during the same time period. In fact, he and the Iceman could even have known each other. Their stories are so similar that they almost match. When the pieces are fit together, they form a rational hypothesis that will be explored. This hypothesis is controversial, but ignoring evidence from so many connections would be a disservice to the science of archaeology and the ancient history recorded in the Bible.

As frustrating as this may sound, in science it is rare for a theory to be proved beyond any possible doubt. When we go beyond empirical evidence—beyond those things we can see, touch, smell, or hear and directly measure—we rely on theoretical and anecdotal evidence to deduce answers. What we are doing is building a case with circumstantial evidence.

We all know the sun is 93 million miles away, based on strong evidence, numerous tests, and a consensus among experts. These only support our assumption that the sun is indeed 93 million miles away. Yet, with all this evidence, we still have not achieved irrefutable proof. I simply say this to emphasize the value of circumstantial evidence. The quantity and quality of evidence only build up the hypothesis to a degree of proof, and that level is short of absolute proof. With this in mind, let's approach this study like a trial, and you can be the judge. Could the body of the Iceman actually be the body of Cain, the firstborn son of Adam and Eve?

Chapter 2

Raising Cain

ONE HAS TO wonder what would motivate a person to make this type of connection between a recently found ancient mummy and a well-known biblical figure. After all, most people would think the chances of proving this far-fetched idea impossible. To be quite honest, I'm the type of person who craves simplicity: I love facts, I love history, and I love the truth. I consider myself analytical and objective and get great satisfaction from arranging all those messy little details of history into their proper order; I have little regard for speculation or opinions. I never would have suggested such an outlandish proposition as this without an abundance of hard facts and strong evidence.

This idea first crossed my mind after reading a newspaper article about the "curse of the Iceman." I had spent fifteen years researching and compiling the chronology of human history, beginning at the creation of Adam. When I worked on the life of Cain, I noticed there was a sevenfold curse on this man recorded in the Bible. Interestingly enough, seven people who were involved with the discovery and study of the Iceman had died in a relatively short time after encountering the mummy.

Now, please bear with me. I'm not trying to sell you on some hocus-pocus, spooky ghost story. I simply am saying that this seemed rather odd and caught my attention. I also realized from my history studies that the carbon dating of the Iceman and the time frame of Cain's life were extremely close. These two facts compelled me to dig deeper into this subject.

As I began to study the articles about the Iceman and the information about Cain, I found numerous correlations. I started to compile all this information. The more I studied, the more evidence I found to support my suspicion. I have found that much of the record we have of Cain mirrors the facts we have discovered about the Iceman. And the more I learned, the more deeply I realized that this body possessed a secret.

I have been reluctant to write about this for several years because just the mention of a curse troubles many people, myself included. People are reluctant to even discuss such things. What has always been a mystery to me is the passage in the Bible (read in the original Hebrew) where God said that anyone finding and slaying Cain would be avenged seven times. Did God really say that? Did He really mean that seven other people would die if they had something to do with finding and slaying this one man? This just did not add up, and I knew there must be something more—something I was missing. This question persisted: was there something that connected the "finding of Cain" to the "finding of the Iceman"?

The Bible says the fear of the Lord is the beginning of wisdom. I am not afraid of a curse from any man, but the curse of God is something I take seriously. After all, the pain of childbirth and working by the sweat of your brow are curses we live with each day.

I decided I would set aside any preconceived notions I held about Cain as a legendary figure and view him as a real person who walked this earth just like you and me.

© *Putting a Face on the Legend of Cain.* Artwork by O. Thomas

Though I cannot claim with absolute certainty that the Iceman is Cain, I invite you to take a good look at all the circumstantial evidence, weigh the facts, and then draw your own conclusion, just as I have. If a detective or a forensic scientist were trying to identify a dead body, what would he be looking for? He would want to answer critical questions such as these: When did this man die? What was the murder weapon? Does the body have any tattoos or identifying marks? Do we have a witness who will testify? And is there corroborating evidence such as DNA or chemical analysis that will match that of the deceased? It is amazing to see how every piece of a puzzle will make the picture a little clearer. Let us overlay the life of Cain onto the body of Otzi the Iceman and see if there is a match.

Now, I want to take you back—way back—several thousand years. I will begin by addressing the historical time frame of Cain and the Iceman. The approximate date for the Iceman's death is revealed by his carbon dating. I would like to briefly address the fact that most Christians and many reputable scientists do not trust C-14 dating when it comes to extremely old dates exceeding 6,000 years, because on the whole, these dates are merely assumptions. Although none of us know for certain how old the earth is, it is irrational to conclude that it is millions or billions of years old when there is no explicit proof.

The Nobel Prize–winning scientist Willard Libby, who invented carbon dating, made an interesting statement about C-14 methods in his 1960 article titled "Radiocarbon Dating":

> The first shock Dr. Arnold and I had was when our advisors informed us that history extended back only to 5,000 years. We had thought initially

that we would be able to get samples all along the curve back to 30,000 years, put the points in, and then our work would be finished. You read statements in books that such and such a society or archeological site is 20,000 years old. We learned rather abruptly that these numbers, these ancient ages, are not known accurately. (Libby, 1960)

In agreement with Libby's statement, I believe C-14 methods become unreliable when the dating goes much further than 5,000 to about 6,000 years back. Luckily, we are in the ballpark here, because several carbon-dating tests have placed the Iceman's death at somewhere between 5,350 and 5,100 years ago (Rollo et al., 2002). Going by the latter number of years (5,100) works out to be about the year 3092 BC. It would be interesting to see if other dating methods support this time frame.

The only record giving the date for Cain's death is found in *The Book of Jubilees,* chapter 4:31, where it says, "Cain died the same year as Adam," 930 years after the creation of man, on the last year of the nineteenth Jubilee (Lumpkin, 2006). Jubilees are forty-nine-year counts, so the calculation would be as follows: 49 x 19—1 = 930 years after creation. We subtract one year because it happened in that year, not after. This is the year 3074 BC, according to Ussher's *Annals of the World* biblical chronology (Ussher, 1658).

So, the Iceman's death in 3092 BC and Cain's death in 3074 BC are only eighteen years apart. A difference of a hundred years is considered a bull's-eye as far as carbon dating is concerned.

From a biblical standpoint, this is amazing: we have the actual body of a man who walked the earth when Adam was still alive! Furthermore, it would mean the Iceman was a comparatively close relative of Adam.

The next important point I want to clarify is why I think Cain's body still would be around some 5,000-plus years after he died. When we carefully examine the curse God put on Cain, we realize that Cain's body would never decompose and return to the ground, as is nature's normal course. Ashes to ashes and dust to dust is the way of all mankind, and being only natural, the body should return to the ground. Genesis 4:11, Young's Literal Translation, says, "and now, cursed art thou from the ground, which hath opened her mouth to receive the blood of thy brother from thy hand."

The Ancient Book of Jasher 1:31 gives the same account but is a little more specific when it says Cain would not be buried in the earth: "cursed be thou from the ground which opened its mouth to receive thy brother's blood from thy hand, and wherein thou didst bury him" (Johnson, 2008).

Interpretation of this passage requires that Cain's body, having been cursed from the ground, could not be buried in the ground like that of his brother Abel. (Keep in mind that Abel was the first person to be murdered and was hidden in the ground by Cain.) It is true that the curse meant the ground would no longer produce food for Cain and he would be a vagabond roaming the earth. The fact is inescapable; however, Cain could not be buried in the earth, for the ground would not open its mouth for him as it did for his brother Abel.

Another statement from the Bible supports the idea that Cain would never return to the ground. Cain makes this statement to God after the curse has been placed upon him: "Behold, thou hast driven me out this day from the face of the ground; and from thy face shall I be hid" (Genesis 4:14, KJV).

Cain, by making this unusual statement, reveals further details of his curse. Because there is no correction from God, the statement is acknowledged to be part of the curse, "thou hast driven me out this day from the face of the ground; and from thy face shall I be hid." Aside from the spiritual implications of separation from God, what would the physical application of "driven from the face of the ground" mean? Could it be that Cain would be hidden away in an icy tomb, and his body would never be returned to the ground? We get a haunting image of this when we see how the Iceman emerged from his frozen tomb. When the ice melted around the Iceman's body, the body appeared to be rising out of a pool. The police report actually said, "it is practically standing up in the ice" (Fowler, 2000). It was almost as if the body were being driven out of the ice.

When I think about Cain saying he would be driven from the face of the ground and look at how the Iceman emerged from the ice encasement, having never entered the earth, it makes an eerie likeness. This more precise meaning found in the Scripture is not an obstacle if we acknowledge the fact that when we do not take the Bible literally, we can actually misinterpret it.

If God truly was saying that Cain was cursed from the ground that opened up to take Abel's body and he would be driven from the face of the ground, then what can we believe happened to Cain's body? All I can say is that it definitely sounds as though Cain's body would still be preserved somewhere in the world, because his body could not decompose; otherwise, he would return to the ground.

Likewise, the Iceman was never buried and is far too precious a discovery to science to ever let decompose. Now that he is a museum artifact, his corpse will never be buried in the ground. In fact, a high-tech refrigerated vault has been created especially for the preservation of his body (South Tyrol Museum of Archaeology, 2011). And if science has its way, he will never be laid to rest; he will be preserved indefinitely.

© *Iceman on Display in His Vault.* Artwork by O. Thomas

Chapter 3

The Way of Cain

HE FOUNDATION OF this book is based on the biblical figure Cain, with a firm understanding that the Bible is God's Word. Several other ancient Hebrew historical documents, which support the biblical account of Cain, are also used to study Cain's life. These Hebrew books are viewed as ancient scripture and history, not sacred or spiritual Scripture, and are not valued at the same level as the Bible. More detail about these ancient manuscripts is provided in the Ancient Historical Records of Cain addendum found in the back of this book.

So what do we know of Cain? Cain was the first human ever born on the earth. He lived approximately 5,100 to 5,900 years ago in the Middle East. Although the original record of Cain comes from the book of Genesis, numerous other ancient Hebrew accounts describe him in great detail, the most notable being *The Antiquities of the Jews* by Josephus and *The Ancient Book of Jasher.*

The consensus among these ancient records paints a picture of a vile degenerate consumed with unbridled, selfish lust. Before Cain murdered his brother Abel, God warned him that sin was crouching at his door and, if he did not resist, would possess him. Apparently, this is what happened, because from that point on, we see a man possessed with greed, envy, and violence.

When Adam and Eve were cast out of Eden, they returned to the land of Adam's creation. Hebrew tradition tells us Adam was created on Mount Moriah, in what later became the site of Jerusalem. Cain would have been born near that location, according to this tradition. Cain is recorded in the Bible to be the first child of Adam and Eve, followed later by his brother Abel and many other siblings. He was a farmer, a tiller of the ground, like his father. His younger brother Abel was a keeper of sheep, a shepherd.

Most people are familiar with the story of Cain and Abel; it is centered on sibling rivalry, jealousy, and the first murder ever committed. What most people do not

The First Murder. Artwork by Gustave Dore

know, however, is what happened to Cain afterward. They do not know that according to ancient history, Cain lived approximately 800 more years and became the father of every evil practice upon the earth.

After Cain murdered his brother, he was cursed by God to become a wanderer throughout the earth. Cain became a fugitive on the run and lived in fear of God and man. He first journeyed eastward from Mount Moriah into the land of Nod. The meaning of the word *Nod* is "to wander or to be lost," so Cain and his progeny became nomads in the land of the lost. There is no information about where Cain might have traveled beyond the land of Nod, but his journeys must have been extensive to earn him the title of "wanderer." We do find in Josephus's account that Cain traveled to distant lands. It says, "And when Cain had traveled over many countries, he, with his wife, built a city, named Nod, which is a place so called, and there he settled his abode; where also he had children." (Whiston, 1987), suggesting Cain never again lived in the region of his birth (the area we now call Israel). The Bible does not indicate Cain ever returned from his exile, but the Book of Jubilees and the Ancient Book of Jasher both mention Cain did return for his father Adam's burial.

According to the Bible, Cain was disrespectful toward God. He lied to God's face when he said he did not know where Abel was after having murdered him. He caused his parents immeasurable amounts of grief by killing his brother, being cursed by God, and (as tradition claims) kidnapping his sister Awan and forcing her to become his wife.

It actually took Adam and Eve approximately thirty-two years of mourning (four shabua of years and four years) before they had another child. A shabua in Hebrew means seven years, so the calculation is as follows: four times seven equals twenty-eight, and four additional years equals thirty-two years, according to *The Book of Jubilees,* before they knew each other again and bore their third son, Seth (Lumpkin, 2006).

© *The Weathered Face of the Iceman.* Artwork by O. Thomas

Several documents describe God placing a curse on Cain. He cursed Cain from the ground that received Abel's body, saying the ground would not produce food for him anymore and that his body would not return to the ground like Abel's. The Bible also says Cain would be hidden from the face of God. According to many books, Cain feared after he killed his brother that anyone finding him would want to kill him.

Because of this, God placed markings on Cain's body, warning that anyone who was involved in finding and smiting him would suffer from a sevenfold curse.

According to *The Book of Jubilees,* Cain wandered and pillaged for hundreds of years before he settled down in the latter years of his life and built a city (Lumpkin, 2006). Cain named the city Enoch, after his firstborn son. *The Antiquity of the Jews* says he divided land and became the creator of measures and weights (Whiston, 1987). This means he was the first person to claim ownership over property and develop a monetary or trading system between his offspring.

He ruled over his family and forced them to stay within the city walls. Even after having children, Cain grew increasingly evil and taught his family to follow in his footsteps. *The Antiquities of the Jews* also says the following about him:

> Nay, even while Adam was alive, it came to pass that the posterity of Cain became exceedingly wicked, every one successively dying, one after another, more wicked than the former. They were intolerable in war and vehement in robberies; and if any one were slow to murder people, yet was he bold in his profligate behavior, in acting unjustly, and doing injuries for gain (Whiston, 1987).

CHRONOLOGY OF THE LIFE OF CAIN

Following is a time line and genealogy of Cain's life based on the Jubilee year cycles found in *The Book of Jubilees*. When it comes to the time spans found in the Bible, everyone seems to have their own opinion. Many researchers conclude there is a time span of roughly 6,000 years from creation to the present, but I have seen estimates all over the board, going back as far as 10,000 or even 20,000 years. The Jubilee chronology and the Ussher chronology differ by about sixty years, so the years given in this chronology should be seen as estimates derived from generally accepted time frames found in the Bible:

» Cain was born when Adam was sixty-nine, in ~3873 BC. *The Book of Jubilees* chapter 4:1 states, "And in the third week in the second jubilee she gave birth to Cain."

» Cain slew Abel in ~3844 BC, when Cain was twenty-nine and Abel was twenty-two. Adam would have been ninety-eight. *The Book of Jubilees* chapter 4:2 states, "And in the first year of the third jubilee, Cain slew Abel."

» Cain was 126 when he took Awan and made her his wife in ~3747 BC. *The Book of Jubilees* chapter 4:9 states, "And Cain took Awan his sister to be his wife at the close of the fourth jubilee."

» After Cain took Awan, he continued to wander; his first habitation was eastward in the land of Nod. Later in his life, he had a son, settled down, and built a city. *The Book of Jubilees* chapter 4:9 states, "Cain built a city, and called its name after the name of his son Enoch."

» Cain died in the same year as his father, Adam, ~3012

BC Adam was 930 and Cain was 861 when he died. *The Book of Jubilees* chapter 4:29–31states, "And at the close of the nineteenth jubilee, in the seventh week in the sixth year thereof, Adam died, and all his sons buried him in the land of his creation …At the close of this jubilee Cain was killed after him in the same year."

Genealogy of Cain

» Adam was the father of Cain, Abel, Awan (his daughter), Seth, Azura (his daughter), and many other children.

» Cain was the father of Enoch.

» Enoch fathered Irad.

» Irad was the father of Mehujael.

» Mehujael fathered Methusael.

» Methusael was the father of Lamech.

» Lamech fathered seventy-seven children, including Jabal, Jubal, Tubal, and Naamah (his daughter).

One must be careful not to confuse the descendants of Cain with the descendants of Seth, because the two lines share similar names. Both lines of descendants have an Enoch and a Lamech, but these are different people. There is also a similarity in the names of Methuselah and Methusael.

A glance at Cain's life reveals that he is not the type of man any normal, law-abiding citizen would want to have over for dinner. The way of Cain is described in the book of Jude (from the Bible) as a path that would lead to destruction for many people, as it did for his children. The way of Cain is murderous, envious, gluttonous, lustful, prideful, greedy, and deviancy that would be classified as insane by any normal terms. Sadly, Cain passed down his traits even to the last of his descendants who died in the flood.

After reading this description of Cain's life, the foundation has been set to build upon this study. These quotes from the actual historical records can be found in the full texts provided in the addendum at the end of the book. I suggest reading the quotes now to get a general understanding of the material we will be discussing.

Now that we have established this background information I would like to take the ancient records of Cain and contrast them with the modern records of the Iceman. The following chapters will begin connecting the history, archaeological findings, and scientific data compiled that link the Iceman to Cain. It is time to examine the remarkable parallels between the two.

Chapter 4

The Markings

OTHER THAN THE timing of their deaths and the fact that their bodies would never return to dust, there would have to be something more tangible linking the Iceman and Cain. There must be something that would solidify the connection, something unique to the body of Cain and only Cain that would pinpoint him in history. What evidence exists that connects these two people? This would be an implausible idea if not for an unmistakable piece of information found in the Bible. The most profound evidence connecting the Iceman to Cain is found in the book of Genesis, where it says Cain's body was marked. The Bible says God marked Cain with a sign. The sign placed on Cain would identify him so that anyone who found him could avoid the curse God had placed on him.

The Iceman's body is indeed marked with fifty-seven symbols

(Gaivin, 2009), assumed to be tattoos, on his back, legs, and arm. The face of the Iceman is so discolored that no facial markings have yet been identified. Scientists who have studied these marks say these were not made using the traditional tattoo method of needle and ink but were incisions filled with charcoal fragments resulting in a black scar (Bahn, 2009).

An article from 2009 in *Discovery News* reads, "The 57 tattoos sported by Otzi, the 5,300-year-old Tyrolean iceman mummy, were made from fireplace soot that contained glittering, colorful precious stone crystals" (Viegas, 2009). Scientists say most of these tattoos are found in the connective tissue rather than the epidermis, and some of the crystals are silica crystals, such as almandine and quartz, whereas others are undefinable (Pabst et al., 2009). Furthermore, the location of many of the markings means they could not have been made by the Iceman himself; someone else engraved them onto Otzi's body. The Bible tells us God marked Cain: Genesis 4:15 says, "And the Lord said to him, 'Therefore, whoever kills Cain, vengeance shall be taken on him sevenfold.' And the Lord set a mark on Cain, lest anyone finding him should kill him."

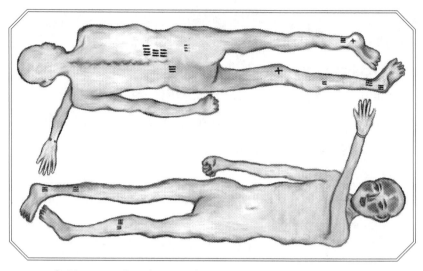

© *Placement of Markings on the Iceman.* Artwork by A. McHale

The word translated as "mark" in this Scripture is the Hebrew word *oth,* which also means "omen, sign, witness, or evidence" (Biblos.com, n.d.). God set the mark(s) on Cain as an omen, a sign to others, and as evidence so that those who found him would know who he was. Coincidentally, the body of the Iceman is marked with a symbol that has the same meaning. Is it a coincidence that the body of the Iceman is marked with the Hebrew letter *tav*? The meaning of the letter *tav* is a well-known Hebrew word that denotes a mark and a sign (Ancient Hebrew Research Center, 1999). In ancient Hebrew script, *tav* was written as an *X*. Scientists refer to these tattoos as the "cruciform marks" on the Iceman (Spindler, 1996).

© Illustration of Tav *X* tattoos found on Otzi. Artwork by O. Thomas

The body also is marked with the Hebrew letter *vav,* which is the sixth letter of the Hebrew alphabet and stands for the number *6.* The word *vav* means a "peg, nail, or hook" (Ancient Hebrew Research Center, 1999). Although *vav* stands for the number *6,* it looks similar to our numeral *1.* It is written with a single downward stroke of the pen. This letter is slightly rounded at the top (certain variations also have a small circle on the top). The Iceman has *vav* marks all over his body, mostly placed in sets of three. There appears to be at least eight sets of *vav-vav-vav* (*666*) marks, more than any other symbol found on the body.

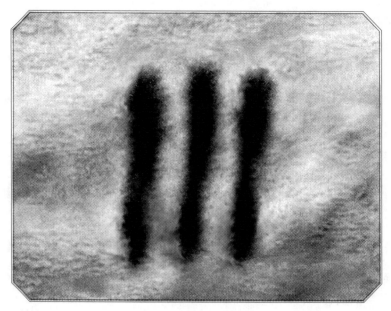

© Illustration of Vav *I* tattoos found on Otzi. Artwork by O. Thomas

This is an extraordinary coincidence, because *666* is the infamous mark of the beast spoken of in the book of Revelation. The number *6* is said to be the number of man because man is imperfect and man was created on the sixth day. Revelation goes further to say the mark of the beast will be the number of a man. The suggestion is that the number of a man is the "number of man," specifically the number *6,* and that it will be a man notoriously known to be marked with this number. So, we see that the Iceman is marked not only with the mark of a sign from God but also with the mark of the beast *666,* which resembles the claw marks of a wild animal. As I searched for ancient documents that might include physical detail about Cain, I came across one book that had a possible description. In the ancient Hebrew mystic book called the *Zohar,* we find the only other reference of what the mark of Cain might have looked like:

Zohar, Vol. 1, Beresheet A, Section 48:458 says, "And Hashem set a mark upon Kayin (Cain) lest anyone finding him should smite him. This is one of the 22 letters of the Torah." The rabbinic commentary in the Zohar says, "which is the letter vav" (Kabbalah Centre International, Inc., 2004).

I am in no way promoting the book of *Zohar,* as it is a mystical book, but am saying rabbinical scholars were aware the mark of Cain was a letter of the Hebrew alphabet. This conclusion likely came from sources lost to our time but recorded in ancient rabbinic writings. Rabbinic traditions going back over a thousand years have said the mark was one of the four letters that spell the name of God "yod", "heh", "vav", "heh;" These ancient Rabbis loved puzzles and cryptic messages. They seemed to enjoy hiding their knowledge so anyone seeking their wisdom would be forced to study in order to solve the problem. In order to solve which of the three letters was the mark of Cain they would have to know the symbolic meaning of the letters. Since the letter "yod" was a hand it symbolically meant to help or work. The letter "heh" symbolically was a jubilant man and meant to celebrate or behold a wonderful thing. We are left with the letter "vav" symbolically a peg meaning to set or affix, which agrees with the Biblical statement "God set a mark on Cain." When you stop and think about the fact ancient writers cryptically identified the mark of Cain as the letter *vav,* and the body of the Iceman has the letter *vav* engraved on it, you must admit this appears to be more than a mere coincidence.

In addition to the X and I marks, the Iceman has one more significant mark engraved on his body. Around his left wrist he has a bracelet-shaped tattoo etched into his flesh. This marking is formed by two parallel lines that go around the wrist but do not completely encircle it. The marking could be described as the shape of a bracelet that is pushed down over the wrist rather than a circular bracelet the hand would pass through. If I had to convey in writing or draw what this mark looked like, the only way I could depict this shape would be to draw a bracelet in the shape of the letter C.

In our day and age we could include a picture to show anyone what this mark looks like, but ancient writers did not have that sophistication. They used simple yet precise symbols to convey a mental picture of the subject. This marking is obviously not a symbol that would be easily recognized, and I think the fact that it is hidden in plain sight makes this a significant discovery.

The Iceman has the symbol C engraved around his wrist, which in the ancient Hebrew alphabet is the letter *Lamed. Lamed* gives the phonic sound "la" or "le" and symbolically represents an ox goad, a device used to control livestock. Because a goad had a sharp pointed spike on the end, the symbol *Lamed* also had a verb form meaning "to pierce the skin."

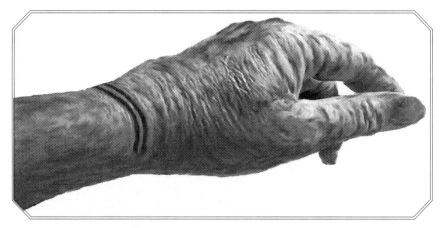

© Illustration of the Iceman's wrist tattoo. Artwork by O. Thomas

The three letters written on the body are Proto-Sinaitic; this is the oldest written consonantal alphabet and the beginning of the Hebrew written language. Hebrew tradition says this language was used before the Tower of Babel and all the way back to the time of Adam. The oldest Proto-Sinaitic inscriptions found so far date to 1900 BC. These inscriptions were discovered in Upper Egypt but were not Egyptian writings, because these symbols came from Semitic-speaking people living in Egypt at that time ("Alphabet, Hebrew," 2012). A study of biblical chronology reveals 1900 BC as the time frame of Abraham's journey into Egypt; this gives us scriptural confirmation that Hebrew people were indeed in Egypt at this point in history.

Let's recap: we have the oldest intact human body ever discovered, a man who perished about the same time as Adam and his son Cain; the body has an image on it that means "a mark and a sign"; and it also has the number *666* embedded deep into the flesh in numerous places. These markings are made with the oldest-known written language, ancient Proto-Sinaitic Hebrew.

Proto-Sinaitic Hebrew Alphabet

© *Ancient Alphabet.* Artwork by O. Thomas

Chapter 5

Geographical Locations

W HEN I FIRST began to consider the connection between Cain and Otzi, I quickly rejected the whole idea because Otzi was found in, of all places, northern Italy. I must admit I tried to set the whole idea aside, but the other connections were too compelling to ignore. One piece of research that caught my attention had to do with Otzi's mobility, or walking pattern. Biologist Christopher Ruff used CT scans to take measurements of the Iceman's skeletal structure. He discovered Otzi was muscular, and his shinbones were larger than normal, especially from front to back. This was an indication that Otzi's way of life included "long walks over hilly terrain." Ruff said that the extent of his mobility was not a trait found in the bones of other Copper Age Europeans (Ruff et al., 2006).

So, the amount of walking Otzi did was much more than normal. The notion that he walked a tremendous amount throughout his lifetime fit the bill, but was there any evidence that tied him to the Middle East? Were there any ancient records of Cain's travels?

We know Cain had a reputation for being a wanderer. *The Ancient Book of Jasher* says, "thou shalt be moving and wandering in the earth until the day of thy death" (Johnson, 2008). Also Flavius Josephus wrote, "Cain had traveled over many countries" (Whiston, 1987). Coincidentally, if you visit the South Tyrol Museum Website and look at the research milestones, you will see a study with this title: "The Iceman's constitution was athletic; he was more a wanderer than a manual worker" (South Tyrol Museum of Archaeology, 2011). Realizing there might be a correlation here, I started searching for more information about where Cain might have traveled after he became a fugitive from the land of his birth.

Try as I might, I could find nothing, not even a hint of where Cain might have roamed during the next 800 years of his life. We can speculate he might have lived in Jericho or Damascus, because the oldest houses to be found on earth are built there. Alas, the trail runs cold, and all we can say with any certainty is that Cain lived somewhere outside the area we now call Israel.

Most people would think that because Cain was born in the Middle East, he would spend his entire life in that region. It has been a basic assumption that the people mentioned in the Bible lived in the area roughly between Mount Ararat and Egypt.

This is the case for most of the Hebrew people, but before the flood, people separated into clans that migrated in every direction. Therefore, the idea that people stayed in the Middle East during the time Cain lived is a misconception.

We know mankind had extended his domain to the far corners of the earth before the deluge, and evidence of this habitation is found from the windswept mountains of Peru to the green hills of Japan. Proof humans were well advanced can be seen in the amazing megalithic structures still standing around the world; Stonehenge is just one example from this pre-flood society.

An interesting discovery recently was made at Stonehenge. In an ancient burial site dated approximately 2500 BC, the skeletal remains of a man were unearthed. Archaeologists determined he was not a native of England but had migrated from the region of the European Alps (Fitzpatrick, 2011). We do know Cain traveled across many lands during his life, and the discovery of this man at Stonehenge indicates that distant journeys were not that unusual.

Along these same lines of thinking is the notion that people would not, or could not, travel great distances from where they were born in ancient times. Dispelling this perception, we have evidence of the use of sailing ships from 3000 BC and earlier. Additionally, flourishing trade routes had extended all the way to China by 2000 BC.

Just recently scientists were able to determine that Otzi did, in fact, travel long distances in short periods of time. By studying the pollens and mosses found with Otzi's body, scientists were able to determine where he traveled in the final days of his life. An article in *National Geographic News* titled "Wounded Iceman Made Epic Final Journey, Moss Shows" reveals how these discoveries were made:

> Together with pollen and cereals found in his gut, the moss is helping scientists piece together the route that Otzi took in his last days of life. They now know that he came from high in the mountains, then went down to the lowlands—where he picked up the bog moss—then returned to the highlands, covering a distance of at least 37 miles (60 kilometers) in two or three days. Despite his relatively advanced age for the time, he was a very fit man and obviously used to going up and down hills, experts say (Ravilious, 2008).

Even though we cannot find specific information to indicate Cain traveled to the region we now call northern Italy, there is likewise no information to suggest he did not. Italy could be the place Cain decided to settle during his later years. When you live for 861 years, a trip from the Middle East to Italy is a relatively short journey. I concluded I could not rule out the possibility of Cain wandering into Italy.

Conversely, the fact that the Iceman died in northern Italy does not exclude the possibility that he migrated there from another location. I wanted to see if there was anything that would connect the Iceman to the location of present-day Israel.

After several months of researching scientific journals on Otzi, I still was unable to find a connection. I began pulling up scientific research on Otzi written in Italian and having it translated. I never will forget the day I came across the link: my mouth dropped open as I read that a scientist had found forensic evidence that indicated the Iceman may have traveled to the Red Sea.

During an archaeological conference celebrating the tenth anniversary of discovering the Iceman, Franco Rollo of the Department of Biology at the University of Camerino, Italy, announced that an unusual bacteria had been discovered in Otzi: *Epulopiscium fishelsonii,* a giant bacterium, was discovered inside Otzi's intestines. This bacteria lives only in the intestines of the surgeonfish (*Acanthurus nigrofuscus*), and the bacteria exists only in the surgeonfish who live in the Red Sea. This was the first time this bacterium had been found in human intestines (Aquaron, 2008). The bacteria were large enough to see with the human eye, about the size of the period at the end of this sentence.

We really have only a few choices when seeking answers about how this bacterium from the Red Sea could have made its way into Otzi's body: either Otzi was in the region of the Red Sea and ate an infected fish, or the Red Sea came to Otzi and he caught the fish near his home in the Italian Alps. There is also a remote third possibility that someone brought the fish to Otzi.

Some scientists have favored the explanation that the Red Sea came to Otzi because it is "inconceivable" to them that he could have traveled to the Red Sea and could have lived in other places. Instead of stating the obvious—Otzi traveled to the Red Sea—these scientists believe the Red Sea must have breached the Sinai Peninsula and the aquatic life migrated to the region of the Alps (Aquaron 2008). They back up the assertion with this theory: The Mediterranean Sea was formed from the primeval sea of Tethys, called the Alpine Ocean. This portion of the Tethys opened in the Lower Cretaceous period between modern-day Europe and the Adria plate near the Southern Alps.

Even though they believe the Cretaceous period was 145 million years to 65 million years ago, they assume the same thing must have happened again approximately 5,000 to 6,000 years ago; otherwise, what else would explain how this bacterium could be found in Otzi's body? They apparently are satisfied with this rationalization to the extent that they never even consider the possibility that Otzi might have been in the area of the Red Sea shortly before his death.

Nevertheless, not everyone agrees with this unlikely theory. After all, are we supposed to believe that tropical coral fish thrived in the area of the Italian Alps? This hypothesis is not convincing to all scientists, and it remains a controversial issue. In my own opinion, having to envision the Red Sea overflowing in order to bring this fish to Otzi strikes me as a little far-fetched.

This bacterium gives us strong physical evidence that the Iceman might have traveled to the region of the Red Sea at some point not too long before his death. Could it be that the

Iceman—i.e., Cain—returned to the land now called Israel for the funeral of his father, Adam? Cain's journey to the Middle East for Adam's funeral is mentioned in *The Book of Jubilees* chapter 4:29: "And at the close of the nineteenth jubilee, in the seventh week in the sixth year thereof, Adam died, and all his sons buried him in the land of his creation, and he was the first to be buried in the earth" (Lumpkin, 2006).

The statement that Adam was the first to be buried in the earth suggests that Abel's body was never found. Hebrew tradition indicates that Adam was prepared for burial and entombed in a cave.

We see it says that "all" of Adam's sons attended his burial, and this of course would have included Cain. If, indeed, Cain went to bury his father, he easily could have eaten or acquired this type of fish for his return journey. In current geography, Israel's southern border is on the Red Sea's Gulf of Aqubah. *The Book of Jubilees* goes on to say that shortly after Adam was buried, Cain died that same year.

This is the clincher for me, because even though we find no evidence that Cain might have traveled to the region we now call Italy, we do have good evidence that both Cain and the Iceman left their homeland and traveled to a location at or near the Red Sea shortly before they died. Cain traveled there to attend his father's funeral shortly before he died, and we have physical evidence that the Iceman traveled there and consumed a fish from the Red Sea shortly before he died.

Is it reasonable to think that a Neolithic man could walk the distance between the areas we now call northern Italy and

Israel? As the crow flies this would be approximately 1,750 miles, from the *Stele di Otzi* (the Otzi monument marking where he was found) to the Gulf of Aqaba in the Red Sea. The distance increases to approximately 2,000 miles following the land route (Google Earth, 2012). A man walking an average of twenty miles per day would require a hundred days, or three months and ten days. If an individual made this voyage by sailboat with favorable winds, it would take twenty days.

In our modern age, walking twenty miles a day might sound like a horrendous undertaking, but it was fairly common throughout history; consider the Crusades, for example, when thousands of men traveled from northern Europe to the Holy Land, in most cases by foot. Would this type of journey be characteristic of a man who was known to wander across many countries? What about a man whose bones reveal a lifestyle of unusually long walks across hilly terrain and who is defined as a wanderer? It's elementary, my dear Watson!

My next question was to look at the area where Otzi was believed to have lived and find out if there was any connection to Cain. The area believed to be the home territory of the Iceman was centered in the vicinity of a Copper Age village called Mount Juval, a stronghold overlook guarding the entrance to the lush Valley of Senales. The region is believed to have been populated since the Stone Age (Haines & McMaster, 1998). This location was so well suited for a fortification that in the twelfth century, Castle Juval was built on this very hill.

© *Castle Juval.* Artwork by A. McHale

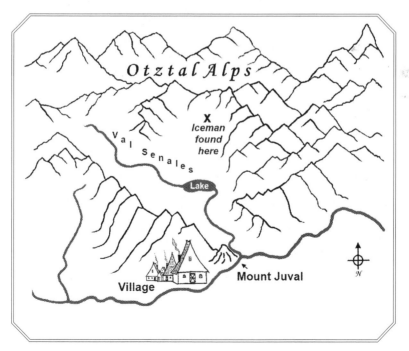

© Map of ancient Stone Age village Juval. Artwork by O. Thomas

In the PBS documentary *Ice Mummies: Return of the Iceman,* archaeologists search for ancient sites close to the location where Otzi was found. Because of its close proximity many archaeologists believe a Stone Age village called Mount Juval was the Iceman's home. The documentary says, "The ancient sites around Castle Juval are only five miles south of where the Iceman was found—close enough to have been his home" (Haines & McMaster, 1998).

The name Juval is intriguing because two of Cain's family members, sons of Lamech, were named Jubal and Tubal. The name Juval is a slight variation of Jubal. Josephus tells us Jubal invented and played musical instruments, and Tubal forged metals. If you read Genesis 4:22 in the original Hebrew it specifically says Tubal-Cain forged copper. Did Cain name this village for a gifted son of his family, and could his brother Tubal be the one who built a furnace at this village to refine metals? It is quite possible Cain himself taught the young men of his family how to melt the chunks of rock containing copper. I say this because the name Cain, or Qayin (קַיִן), meaning "possession" in Hebrew, also has the meaning "smith" as in metalsmith (Biblos.com, n.d.).

Cain also used metal tools to plant and harvest his crops. The Bible and *The Book of Jubilees* both refer to Cain as a tiller of the ground or worker of the ground. *The Ancient Book of Jasher* reads, "And in some time after, Cain and Abel his brother went one day into the field to do their work; and they were both in the field, Cain tilling and ploughing his ground" (Johnson, 2008).

After the earth stopped producing food for Cain by way of agriculture, did he continue working the ground to extract copper as a means to sustain himself? By comparison, the Iceman was also believed to forge metal. The high levels of arsenic in the Iceman's hair indicate that he was involved in copper smelting (South Tyrol Museum of Archaeology, 2011). Small bits of metal were found under his fingernails, also indicating he was involved in metallurgy. His ax is actually 99.7 percent pure copper (Spindler, 1996). There is a possibility that the ax was forged at Mount Juval. Archaeologists have found evidence that this was the site of copper smelting and stone-tool carving around the same time period Otzi lived.

It is no stretch of the imagination to think that if Cain established another location, such as Mount Juval, he might have named it for another member of his family. We know Cain named a city he built after his son Enoch, as stated in the Bible and also mentioned in *The Book of Jubilees*. Was the notorious name of Cain's lair in the west perpetuated in the minds of Noah and his children, and did this name transcend the flood to be reestablished by Noah's descendants' years later in the same location and retaining the same name, Juval?

Here, too, we have circumstantial evidence not only in the fact that Cain and Otzi both walked great distances in their lives and are both depicted as wanderers but also in the probability that they both traveled to the area near the Red Sea shortly before they died. We also have evidence in metallurgy trades and family names recorded in the ancient records. Interesting, wouldn't you say, Watson? More clues that support a connection between the biblical figure of Cain and the archaeological history of the location where the Iceman lived! Josephus confirms these connections in *The Antiquities of the Jews* when he talks about the great-great-great-grandson of Cain, Lamech, in chapter 2:2:

> Lamech; who had seventy-seven children by two wives, Silla and Ada. Of those children by Ada, one was Jabal: he erected tents, and loved the life of a shepherd. But Jubal, who was born of the same mother with him, exercised himself in music; and invented the psaltery and the harp. But Tubal, one of his children by the other wife, exceeded all men in strength, and was very expert and famous in martial performances. He procured what tended to the pleasures of the body by that method; and first of all invented the art of making brass. (Whiston, 1987)

Chapter 6

5,000-Year-Old
Murder Mystery Solved?

U P TO THIS point, some compelling similarities between the Iceman and Cain have been discussed. Both men would have been alive at the same time, their deaths are estimated to have been extremely close in time, one man's body could not return to the ground and the other man's body never decomposed into the ground, both men had markings tattooed on their bodies, there is a high probability that both men traveled to the Red Sea close to the time of their deaths, and they were both well known for being wanderers. All of these similarities are remarkable, but if any of the evidence could be so precise, so on target, could hit the bull's-eye (so to speak), it would be the way these men were killed. This information could close the case of a 5,000-year-old murder mystery.

Hundreds of articles and Websites speak of the Iceman's murder as though it were an episode of *Bones*. It is referred to as a "paleo crime scene" that is still under investigation (Hall, 2007). It is almost as though every person who studies this body shares a deep conviction that there is more to this mysterious murder, and it keeps them digging for more clues.

In the 1990s, it first was believed that the Iceman might have died from overexposure (Ridge, 2003). However, X-ray images taken in 2001 revealed that he died from an arrowhead that was still embedded in his chest ("Mystery demise of Oetzi iceman is finally solved" 2001). This arrow severed major blood vessels and resulted in a painful but quick death. The entry wound still is visible on the dorsal side of the left shoulder (Gostner, 2002). Otzi now is believed to have died from massive blood loss caused by the wound and to have died rather quickly (Pain, 2001). From the nature of this wound, he probably would have died even if modern medical techniques had been available.

If we investigate the murder of Cain, we might be able to solve the mystery of who shot the arrow that killed the Iceman, because a detailed account of Cain's death given in *The Ancient Book of Jasher* 2:26–31 says that a fatal arrow wound is precisely how Cain died!

> And Lamech was old and advanced in years,
> and his eyes were dim that he could not see,
> and Tubal Cain, his son, was leading him and

it was one day that Lamech went into the field and Tubal Cain his son was with him, and whilst they were walking in the field, Cain the son of Adam advanced towards them; for Lamech was very old and could not see much, and Tubal Cain his son was very young.

And Tubal Cain told his father to draw his bow, and with the arrows he smote Cain, who was yet far off, and he slew him, for he appeared to them to be an animal. And the arrows entered Cain's body although he was distant from them, and he fell to the ground and died. And the Lord requited Cain's evil according to his wickedness, which he had done to his brother Abel, according to the word of the Lord which he had spoken. And it came to pass when Cain had died, that Lamech and Tubal went to see the animal which they had slain, and they saw, and behold Cain their grandfather was fallen dead upon the earth. And Lamech was very much grieved at having done this, and in clapping his hands together he struck his son and caused his death (Johnson, 2008).

When I discovered this, I had to stop and regain my composure. Initially, this was an exciting adventure; researching, studying, and finding new clues had become my hobby for several years, but this was different. Lining up the arrowhead connection made this hypothesis so real that I felt like something supernatural was being revealed to me.

Cain indeed was shot with an arrow by his family members Lamech and Tubal. I remembered the writings of Flavius Josephus saying that God "threatened his (Cain's) posterity in the seventh generation" (Whiston, 1987). I quickly studied the lineage to find which generation Lamech and Tubal belonged to. Sure enough, Lamech was the seventh generation from Adam, and Tubal was the seventh generation from Cain. Flavius Josephus goes on to write that Lamech knew the seventh generation would be part of Cain's curse. He wrote, "And because he (Lamech) was so skillful in matters of divine revelation, that he knew he was to be punished for Cain's murder of his brother, he made that known to his wives" (Whiston, 1987).

The very fact that this murder was an accident makes the story even more credible. Cain really looked like an animal! After Lamech shot Cain, he was so shocked and distraught that he accidentally killed his son Tubal. Imagine the type of untold terror and agony that must have overtaken him in this moment! In the Bible, Genesis 4:23–24 reads as follows:

"And Lamech said unto his wives, Adah and Zillah, Hear my voice; ye wives of Lamech, hearken unto my speech: for I have slain a man to my wounding, and a young man to my hurt. If Cain shall be avenged sevenfold, truly Lamech seventy and sevenfold."

Here we see the Bible revealing Lamech as the one who killed Cain. Seventy and sevenfold, or seventy-seven, is an interesting number because Lamech's two wives bore him seventy-seven children between them.

At this point, I wanted to know if there were any other ancient documents that claimed that Cain was killed by his family. I also needed to know if there were any clues about who killed the Iceman. In addition to *The Ancient Book of Jasher,* which claims Cain was killed by his family members, *The Book of Jubilees* makes a veiled reference supporting this allegation. *The Book of Jubilees* says that Cain was killed when "his house fell upon him," a metaphor for someone being killed by his own family. It also says he died shortly after his father, Adam. *The Book of Jubilees* goes on to say, "he died in the midst of his house and he was killed by its stones." This can be taken metaphorically and literally to mean that he died in front of his family, and that the arrowhead that punctured his artery, making him bleed to death, was a stone found, crafted, and shot by the very hands of his own family.

The Book of Jubilees 4:31: "At the close of this jubilee Cain was killed after him (Adam) in the same year; for his house fell upon him and he died in the midst of his house, and he was killed by its stones; for with a stone he had killed Abel, and by a stone was he killed in righteous judgment" (Lumpkin, 2006).

Shortly after I learned how Cain was killed, I read an article on the murder of Otzi that aligned closely with this ancient account. In a BBC World News article about the Iceman, this information was reported:

After more than 10 years studying the perfectly preserved body, scientists now think he was shot with an arrow which came from the same area as Otzi himself. This small object is at the centre of one of the most extraordinary stories in modern archaeology. It is a perfect replica of the flint arrowhead scientists now think killed Otzi the iceman, the 5,300-year-old hunter who emerged from a melting glacier in the Italian Alps in 1991. A copy has been constructed using data from a 3D computer-aided tomography image ("Iceman probably killed by own people," 2002).

© Iceman Killed by Arrowhead Made by His
Own Clan. Artwork by O. Thomas

How extraordinary that Otzi was believed to be killed by his own kinsmen, just like Cain! It is amazing how advanced forensic science has become. In the Discovery Channel documentary *Iceman: Hunt for a Killer,* experts reenact the shooting of the

Iceman with a handmade replica of a bow and arrow. After extensive research, they conclude Otzi was shot with an arrow from about thirty yards away at a twenty-five-degree down-sloped angle (Goldberg, 2003). This lines up with Lamech and Tubal Cain shooting Cain from afar. If the Iceman was Cain, he certainly would have looked like an animal with all of the animal fur he was wearing when he died.

But what about the "field" *The Ancient Book of Jasher* said Lamech and Tubal were walking in when they shot Cain? Otzi was shot in the mountains, right? There are three scientific findings that lead me to believe that the area where Otzi died might have had grass like a field.

The first clue is that many of Otzi's personal items were made of leather and grasses. Two examples are the soles of his bearskin shoes, which were filled with grasses, and his cape, which was made of woven grasses (Bahn, 2005). There were several different varieties of grasses found with Otzi. Yes, it is probable Otzi made these items in a village below, but that still does not rule out the probability of there being grass where he died. In fact, eighty meters from the location of the find of the Iceman is an ancient crossing called the Tisenjoch (Spindler, 1996). Konrad Spindler describes it in his book *The Man in the Ice:* "It is an ancient crossing from the Val di Senales to the Otztal. Even in the present century it was used as an alternative for driving sheep up to the Alpine pastures whenever unfavorable snow conditions made the steep and difficult southern slope of the neighboring crossings too dangerous" (Spindler, 1996). Here we see the sheep were driven up to the Alpine pastures.

Secondly, we know it was sometime between spring and summer that Otzi ingested the yellow pollen of the hornbeam blossoms (Hall, 2007). Out of any time of year, this would be when we would expect to see flowers and grasses spring forth. And the truth of the matter is that we can only speculate what the climate was like 5,000 years ago and the altitude of the mountain range in that time period.

An article titled "Remains of Grasses Found with the Neolithic Iceman Otzi" examines all of the grasses found at the site.

> Plants that had been growing at the site allow the reconstruction of the local vegetation at the time of the Iceman. The broad course of the vegetation history in the wider surroundings is well known from pollen analytical investigations of mires at high altitudes in the Otz valley region. However, the detailed vegetation changes at the site throughout the Neolithic are unknown. Whether the ground of the gully was covered with vegetation at the precise time of the mummy deposition is still in question. (Acs, Wilhalm, & Oeggl, 2005)

The last clue was found by Dr. Tom Loy on a tool Otzi had with him. When Dr. Loy examined the scraper, he found grass particles on it. "One edge was covered with 'silica gloss,' the polished coating left from cutting grasses which contain large amounts of silica in their tissues. There were even tiny plant hairs embedded in the gloss—evidence that Otzi had been hacking through the grass with this edge" (Loy, 1998). Whether it was to insulate his shoes or to walk through a certain path, Otzi was hacking through grass shortly before he died.

After looking at these facts, I concluded there was no conflict between the ancient account and the location where Otzi was discovered. Another thought is that the author of the ancient book could have used the word *field* as a general term to describe a location where these men went to hunt. Again, there is no definite way to know the altitude of the mountain range at that time or the climate. The only thing we know is that at one moment Otzi was picking leaves and cutting grass, and shortly after he died, it became extremely cold and began to snow.

Possibly the most intriguing aspect of this story is the ferocious fighting believed to have happened before Otzi died. Forensic evidence revealed the Iceman had other wounds on his body, suggesting a brutal fight possibly days before he was murdered. Traces of blood from four different people were found on his weapons and coat (Bahn, 2005).

Whose blood could it have been? There is no doubt that Cain was a seasoned warrior and a notorious murderer. Therefore the blood would likely have been from the last four people who came into contact with Otzi a day or two before he died.

I want to interject here an interesting parallel to one of Otzi's weapons. Otzi's knife was a fearsome weapon with a razor-sharp edge; his bow and arrows were deadly as well. Both the knife and the arrows bore human DNA, suggesting that he used these weapons in battle while he was on the run (Mazza, 2008). His ax, his most formidable weapon, revealed red blood cells only from an animal, along with hair, collagen, and copper oxide (Loy, 1998). Coincidentally, there is a possibility that Cain used a tool just like this to kill Abel. The ax that was found with Otzi is almost identical to the weapon described in *The Ancient Book of Jasher* that was used to kill Abel!

The Bible and *The Book of Jubilees* both refer to Cain as a tiller of the ground. In *The Ancient Book of Jasher* 1:17 and 25, we find this description of how Cain killed his brother:

> And in some time after, Cain and Abel his brother went one day into the field to do their work; and they were both in the field, Cain tilling and ploughing his ground, and Abel feeding his flock. …And Cain hastened and rose up, and took the iron part of his ploughing instrument, with which he suddenly smote his brother and he slew him, and Cain spilt the blood of his brother Abel upon the earth (Johnson, 2008).

The following picture shows examples of Neolithic agricultural tools used for tilling the ground; Otzi's ax is on the right. When a method for refining copper was developed, stone tools were replaced with copper-tip tools.

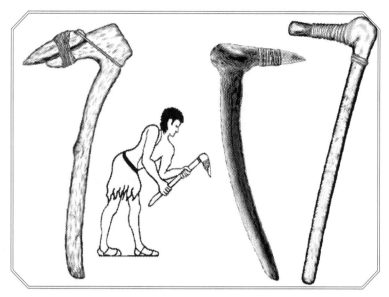

© Neolithic agriculture tools compared with Otzi's
ax (far right). Artwork by O. Thomas

When considering the type of metal-tip tool Cain used to kill Abel, it should be noted that iron had not yet been invented and that copper was the first metal used for tool making. A more accurate translation of *Jasher* probably would have said the *"metal" part of his ploughing instrument to kill his brother.* One cannot help but notice how similar the ax found with Otzi is to the Neolithic tools used for tilling the ground.

It is thought that the Iceman spent his last days on the run. An article in the *Quaternary Science Reviews* summarizes his movements:

During his last 33 or so hours, Otzi crossed different habitats in the Otzal mountains over considerable distances from high up near the timber line (at about 2500m), to low down in the zone of warmth-loving trees (about 1200m or less), and finally very high in the zone of perennial ice (above 3000m). These final journeys lend new weight to the "disaster" theory of Otzi's death, which suggests that, returning from the high alpine pastures to his native village, he came into a severe conflict with his kin such that he had to flee from the community back to the high ground familiar to him, where he died. (Oeggl et al., 2007)

Supporting this theory, the DNA analysis found traces of blood from three different people on his weapons: one from his knife, and two from the same arrowhead (Loy, 1998). A fourth person's blood also was found on his coat. This indicates that Otzi had recently killed, or injured, two people with the same arrow and possibly another person with his knife. The blood on his coat might have been from a fourth victim.

Otzi had numerous wounds in the areas of his hands, wrists, and chest (Bahn, 2005). Additionally, there is evidence of a traumatic injury to the head. One cut to the base of his thumb went down to the bone.

© *The Iceman Puts Moss in His Wounds.* Artwork by O. Thomas

These wounds were from an earlier conflict before the fatal arrow wound, because they had just begun to heal before his death. A report from the Department of Pathology, Academic Hospital Munich-Bogenhausen, in Germany, said, "Our findings indicate that the Iceman sustained a stab wound to the right hand. Besides the site of the arrow wound, there were two other contusions on his back" (Nerlich et al., 2009). Research also indicates that the deadly arrow's shaft had been removed from Otzi's body either just before or soon after he died. From this fact, we can deduce that he either reached back and pulled it out—highly unlikely—or he did not die alone; his murderer was right there but evidently left the scene abruptly, taking none of Otzi's possessions.

What might have been the reason for the murderer leaving the scene without taking the valuable copper ax or the knife? Some scientists believe Otzi was placed in the mountain pass as a ritual sacrifice, but I tend to believe the studies of Frank Rollo, who thinks it was a hunter who killed Otzi and that he died right there:

> Mesolithic deer and wild boar hunters used to aim their arrows and spears at the left shoulder blade as this gave them the best chance of killing the prey at the first shot. As the arrow that struck Otzi actually pierced his left shoulder blade, it seems to us much more reasonable to assume that, rather than of a ritual sacrifice, he had been the victim of some rivalry among big game hunters. (Rollo et al., 2002)

Using the forensic data gleaned from the Iceman's body and the ancient record we have of Cain's death allows me to merge them together to reconstruct a murder scenario:

Cain had been away from his clan for several months and planned to return home soon. For the first time since he had built the village, he traveled back to the land of his birth, because word had reached him that his father, Adam, was dying. It would be the first time the clan had been free from the tormenter who had ruled over them. While Cain was gone, seven of the clan members made a secret pact to kill him when he returned.

They were murderers and thieves who had no regard for human life and crossed every line of decency to please their master. Cain threatened them with the curse from God if anyone should harm him. Although they all desperately desired his death, not one man ever had enough courage to attempt it. Their opportunity came when word reached them that Cain was in the river valley below, about a day's journey from home. So, they planned to attack him together. Seven on one was an achievable task, and if one should bear the curse, they all would.

Lamech did not know their plan. They knew he had poor eyesight and also how terrified he was of Cain's curse. They had heard many times of Lamech's fear that somehow this curse would fall upon him. Because of his poor eyesight, Lamech especially feared Cain and made it a habit to keep his distance from him. Lamech knew Cain was a man who gave no mercy to anyone who offended him.

Telling the rest of the clan they would be away hunting, the seven devised a plan to kill Cain in the valley below. If the mission succeeded, the family would never know what happened to Cain. They would probably think he stayed in the land of his birth.

It was the time of the year when most of the men would leave to hunt ibex in the mountains. Mount Juval sat on the eastern side of the village, and the men gathered there to forge metal tools and carve stone arrow points. All of the men would be at Mount Juval preparing for the hunt while the conspirators headed east into the river valley.

A large stone house overlooked the Val Senales, and this is where all the men gathered to prepare. They carved their flint arrowheads to make them small and efficient, precisely the way Cain had shown them. He passed down the method to each generation so it had become part of their heritage. The stage was set for Cain's house to fall upon him.

By early that evening, the ambushers had spotted Cain. The die was cast and the trap was set, but things went terribly wrong. The plan was to kill Cain with one swift lethal blow to the head as he slept, just as he had killed Abel. Unfortunately, the forceful blow that would have killed most men merely glanced off Cain's skull and turned him into a raging bull. Nothing went according to plan. Cain rose up and fought like a madman.

Bruised and bleeding, one of the men grabbed Cain from behind as another lunged to stab him in the heart, but he managed to block the thrust of the knife with his hand. Blocking the knife saved his life at the cost of a deep wound down to the bone of his right hand. Two attackers held him as the other threw blows to his back. But they were no match for the likes of Cain.

Now, in the dark of the night, two of the attackers lay dead, and two more were wounded critically. Cain was able to escape into the mountains, where he hid out the next day. He was a warrior with an incredibly high tolerance for pain and was still able to provide food for himself with his excellent hunting skills. He filled his wounds with a medicinal moss collected from nearby trees. He knew he had to make it home before his attackers could regroup so he could get the rest of his men to kill these traitors.

But when he quietly crept back to Mount Juval, he found that all the men were gone on the hunt. Not allowing the women and children to see him, he gathered supplies along with fresh meat and bread and headed up to the alpine pastures to find the hunters. Cain had his fur cap and grass coat, which provided perfect camouflage for his entire body. He worked his way high into the pass under the cover of night, leery of his attackers and planning his revenge. After Cain had reached the top of this familiar pass, he took off his weapons and tools, laid them down by a large stone, and tried to get some rest.

By the foggy light of dawn in the distance, he thought he saw what appeared to be two men walking up the hill. They had not seen him, so Cain advanced slowly toward them, crouching in the tall grass and brush like an animal. He was not sure if it was his clan members who would help him or the ones wanting to kill him. From thirty yards away, it still was difficult to tell. Just then, one of the men drew his bow and fired an arrow that just missed Cain's head. Cain turned and ran back up the hill to grab his bow and arrows. But just before he reached them, the sting of a blade tore through the flesh of his back and pierced his subclavian artery. The shot stopped him dead in his tracks. He instantly fell forward to the ground near his belongings and died.

Tubal had directed his father, Lamech, to take the shot. He believed Cain to be an animal, and they hurried up the hill to see their trophy. A look of pure terror fell over Lamech when he realized what they had done. For years, he had been tormented by this man, and all those years he had hung his head in submission for fear of the curse. Now the nightmare had become a reality. All the years of avoiding Cain to protect himself and his family were wasted. How could he have killed this man by mistake?

Tubal rolled the body over to remove the arrow but pulled out only the shaft. Lamech grabbed the arrow from his hand and broke it in two, throwing it on the ground. Then in a blind rage he lashed out at his son, and with one fatal blow sent Tubal tumbling down the hill. Rushing to his son, he picked up his body and carried him back to the village. An icy wind began to blow over the mountain as Lamech struggled to make his way down, leaving Cain's body dead on the ground with all of his tools. Nothing on earth mattered to him anymore. As Lamech walked with his dead son, he ached as though the arrow had pierced his own heart. He had killed this old man to his own wounding and a young son to his hurt (Genesis 4:23).

When he reached the village, the women were mourning over the men who had died in a terrible attack the previous night. Zillah, Tubal's mother, cried out in anguish when she saw her dead son. The remaining conspirators were relieved to hear how Cain had perished and that no one would know what really happened. Some of the clan wanted to retrieve Cain's body, but a violent storm was approaching, and it was too risky to return to the mountain. They were saddened for Lamech, the brother they had all tried to protect. Lamech feared at that point that if Cain was cursed sevenfold, he would be cursed seventy-seven-fold, which would go out unto every last one of his children, as it did Tubal.

The two stories—the forensic evidence found on the Iceman's body and the ancient account of the death of Cain—merge to create a fascinating tragedy with a surprise ending. It happened long ago and far away, yet we might have the answer to the oldest murder mystery on earth. The evidence provided by these ancient books is exhibited on Otzi's body.

An arrowhead fatally pierced both these men. What we have here, Watson, is as close to proof as we will ever have in the mysterious case of the Iceman's murder. The ancient account gives a complete confession by the killer. The verdict is determined to be involuntary manslaughter by way of a hunting accident. Can the 5,300-year-old murder case now be closed? All in all, Cain's death was just recompense for a lifetime of offenses not only against Abel but also many others. Cain's humiliating death—being shot down like a wild animal—brings to mind the old saying, "Those who live by the sword shall die by the sword."

© *Death of the Iceman*. Artwork by O. Thomas

Chapter 7

Antediluvian DNA

Ⓣʜᴇ Iᴄᴇᴍᴀɴ's DNA gives physical evidence of the worldwide flood that almost wiped out mankind. A recent study in *Current Biology* found that the Iceman's mitochondrial DNA apparently is not related to anyone living today. "We found that the Iceman belonged to a branch of mitochondrial haplogroup K1 that has not been identified in modern European populations. This is the oldest complete Homo sapiens mtDNA genome generated to date" (Ermini et al., 2008).

The Iceman's mtDNA does not match up with any of the three known branches K1-A, B, or C (Rollo et al., 2006). In fact, Otzi's DNA is so different from any other DNA found in the world today that it has its own classification: Haplogroup K1-O. The O stands for Otzi, because he is the only member of this classification.

There was a recent study published in 2012 from the *Nature Communications* Journal that has spawned many subsequent articles claiming Otzi has "distant relatives." The DNA sequencing study examined the Y-chromosome, which is passed down from the father's DNA, and categorized Otzi into the Y-haplogroup G2a4. The study also re-examined the mtDNA, mother's DNA, and agreed with the previous study. The article states, "The mitochondrial consensus generated from our data showed 100% concordance with the previously published Iceman mitochondrial genome, underlining the sequence authenticity" (Keller, et al., 2012).

The researchers did find possible links for common ancestors from the father's DNA. The article says, "We found indication for recent common ancestry between the Iceman and present-day inhabitants of the Tyrrhenian Sea (particularly Corsica and Sardinia)..." (2012). This study does not report finding descendants of the Iceman's direct line. These people have similar DNA to Otzi's ancestors, which would be linked through the other children of Adam if the Iceman were Cain. One other report actually speculates that the Iceman may have been sterile, but this is little more than a guess.

Although these discoveries do not provide irrefutable evidence that the Iceman is Cain, the possibility would have been eliminated if the Iceman had direct living descendants, because according to the Bible, Cain's progeny all died in the flood. This also indicates, though not conclusively, that the Iceman was not descended from Noah. On the face of it, the DNA evidence is consistent with that of a man who died before the flood and whose direct line perished during that cataclysm.

The Deluge. Artwork by Gustave Dore

According to biologist Franco Rollo, "This doesn't simply mean that Otzi had some 'personal' mutations making him different from the others but that, in the past, there was a group—a branch of the phylogenetic tree—of men and women sharing the same mitochondrial DNA. Apparently, this genetic group is no longer present" ("Tyrolean Iceman is the end of his line," EU-Cordis 2008). Otzi's DNA, as far as we know, represents an entire branch of the human race that has disappeared off the face of the earth.

Genesis 7:23 says, "And every living substance was destroyed which was upon the face of the ground, both man, and cattle, and the creeping things, and the fowl of the heaven; and they were destroyed from the earth: and Noah only remained alive, and they that were with him in the ark."

This raises a puzzling question: If Cain died before the flood, how could his body have been preserved through this catastrophe? Finding anything of an organic nature from before the flood is rare. At the pyramids, for example, we find hardly any evidence of wood construction; everything appears to be scrubbed down to bare rock. From what we can see, anything organic surviving the flood either was buried deep in the ground or sealed in some type of watertight containment.

In the higher elevations of the western United States, we find bristlecone pine trees that actually predate the flood. Among them, a tree called the Methuselah tree is the oldest living thing on earth, and is more than 4,700 years old (Lorey, 1994), leading me to believe these trees might have been encased in snow and ice for at least part of the flood's duration.

A Christian worldview describes the flood as a completely world-altering event involving massive volcanic activity, earthquakes, and every landmass being moved from its place. Although I do believe the flood caused dynamic atmospheric and geographic changes, I know for a fact that God was able to preserve an object through this cataclysm—an ark constructed of gopher wood and pitch, filled with eight people and numerous species of animals. So the question I pose here is this: Did God have the ability to preserve any object he wanted, such as a glacier, during the worldwide flood? I definitely would say yes.

God is not governed by any of the laws of nature; he created them!

The glacier covering the Iceman provided an encasement that would have protected him in much the same manner as it protected the woolly mammoths we find encased in ice from time to time (Howorth, 1887). The rainfall of the flood could have fallen in the form of a sudden massive snowstorm in the higher latitudes and elevations. Many of these mammoths are found in a standing position with green vegetation still in their mouths (Howorth, 1887). The sudden snow and hailstorm at the start of the flood could have created a phenomenon unlike anything ever seen on earth previously. Balmy temperatures of 80 or 90 degrees could have dropped to a numbing 20 or 30 degrees below zero in a matter of minutes.

© *Woolly Mammoth Frozen While Still Standing.* Artwork by O. Thomas

Knowing this, it is not difficult to imagine how the glacier that covered Otzi would have remained intact for the duration of time that the floodwater totally covered the earth.

One thing I want to reiterate is Genesis 7:23, which reads, "And every living substance was destroyed which was upon the face of the ground." Here we see that God specifically said that everything on the "face of the ground" would be destroyed in the flood. I can see this would mean anything on the surface of the ground leaving the possibility that something buried in the ground or encased in ice could remain intact. In chapter 3 of this book, we read the King James Version of Genesis 4:14, where Cain said, "Behold, thou hast driven me out this day from the face of the ground; and from thy face shall I be hid." Again this unusual statement of Cain's alludes to some sort of concealment or encasement. As the earth raged with torrent and quake, the Iceman remained unaffected, protected in his icy tomb.

Cain did not die in the flood, but all his descendants did, the result of the curse he had brought upon them. Abel, whose life was cut short by Cain, never had the chance to marry nor have children. The Bible tells us his voice was heard beyond the grave asking God for justice. Abel was the first to enter the everlasting life of spirit and soul in the presence of God.

The book of Enoch says Abel made a petition to God that Cain and his evil descendants be held accountable for their deeds. Justice was served in the form of the flood that cleansed the earth of that wicked generation.

Enoch 22:7 says, "And he (the Angel) answered me saying: 'This is the spirit which went forth from Abel, whom his brother Cain slew, and he makes his suit against him till his seed is destroyed from the face of the earth, and his seed is annihilated from amongst the seed of men'" (Nyland, 2010).

Almost every culture in the world today shares the common story of the great flood. The geology of the earth itself tells the story of the flood if one can see past the unreliable machinations of evolution. Instead of finding layers and layers of creatures that have evolved progressively into humans, we find layer upon layer of sedimentary rock with all manner of fossils. Supposedly, these layers represent millions of years of geologic time, and growing up through the middle of all these layers we find a petrified tree. I am not talking about just one tree but literally thousands of these "polystrate," multi-strata, tree fossils, which are found around the world. This is an impossibility according to evolution, because the tree could not have grown for millions and millions of years to be present throughout all these geological ages.

So, how does evolution explain this petrified tree? It does not; it just ignores it and goes along its merry way. The logical explanation is that the tree was growing at the time of the flood and then the layers of sedimentary material formed over a short period of time, burying the tree.

Through the study of DNA, the microscopic world of polymers and nucleotides reveals that all living things are encoded with individual "sets of instructions." These instructions are leading many scientists to reconsider the concept of intelligent design, because you cannot have a set of instructions without them being designed first.

If we have learned anything from studying the 5,300-year-old mummy, it is that humans do not evolve. Otzi's bodily features and functions are exactly the same as modern man's. Oh, but monkeys turned into men over millions or billions of years—no, there is absolutely no way to prove that! However, we can trace the lineage of man all the way back to the creation of Adam, using the Bible and the ancient historical records.

Even in science, all haplogroups can be traced to the first male ancestor of all living humans who rightfully is called "Y-chromosomal Adam." The truth is that no human being knows the actual age of Earth. The millions and billions of years are merely faith-based assumptions—guesses.

What evolutionists have to realize is that the existence of man is based on faith any way you look at it. Evolutionists by default must believe in the supernatural, because a rock or particle of dust at some point supernaturally became a living cell. At some point in time, nonliving matter became living matter, according to evolution. Christians and Jews also believe that at some point nonliving matter became living matter. However, we know the supernatural part to be God. An evolutionist will not attempt to explain how it happened, but will still believe it did. Christians and Jews believe God used the dust to form man and breathed life into him. As Genesis 2:7, King James Version, describes, "Then the Lord

God formed a man from the dust of the ground and breathed into his nostrils the breath of life, and the man became a living being." And that same breath that gave life to Adam is in you and I, this is the breath of life that has been passed down through all generations.

In regard to the creation, I want to reference another intriguing physical anomaly of Otzi: X-ray images revealed that he did not have a twelfth pair of ribs. Material from the South Tyrol Museum says, "Although this is a rare anatomical anomaly, it would not have impaired him in any way" (South Tyrol Museum of Archaeology, 2011). The twelfth set of ribs also are known as "floating ribs" because they are not attached to the sternum, only to the vertebrae of the spine.

Normally, the human skeleton, both male and female, has twenty-four ribs, twelve on each side. In rare cases, people are born missing a set of ribs, and some people can be born with an extra set of ribs. Otzi happens to be one of those rare people missing ribs. The twist is that Adam, Cain's father, is mentioned in the Bible as missing a rib. God took a rib from him to create Eve, as the New King James Version of Genesis 2:20–22 describes:

> So Adam gave names to all cattle, to the birds
> of the air, and to every beast of the field. But for
> Adam there was not found a helper comparable
> to him. And the Lord God caused a deep sleep to
> fall on Adam, and he slept; and He took one of
> his ribs, and closed up the flesh in its place. Then

the rib which the Lord God had taken from man
He made into a woman, and He brought her to
the man.

Could it be that God altered Adam's DNA when he removed
his rib? His rib was taken for the specific replication of his DNA
to form another person. If the Iceman is indeed Cain, and his
father's DNA for a rib was removed and given to Eve, then
there would have been a 50 percent chance that he would have
received a missing-rib trait from Adam (a greater chance if the
missing-rib trait crossed over into Eve).

Adam was the archetype, or original form, of human DNA.
At the time God took Adam's rib, it was to duplicate his DNA to
create the beautiful woman Eve. God taking Adam's rib allowed
for his descendants to have either twelve or eleven sets of ribs.
Likewise, Eve's DNA could have allowed for her descendants
to have eleven, twelve, or thirteen pairs of ribs, which seems
a plausible explanation why sometimes people can have fewer
or more ribs than twenty-four. Still, we cannot escape the fact
that through creation, Adam had a missing rib(s) that was given
to Eve, and his genes could have been altered in this process.
Is it possible Cain's DNA contained genetic information that
would cause him to be missing ribs like his father, and here we
have a man bearing remarkable similarities to Cain, who also
is missing ribs?

In the article "Darwin's Rib," in *Discover* magazine, there
is speculation that creation scientists will make a connection
between the Bible and the body of this ancient mummy. It

reads, "Oh yes, and that 5,300-year-old man they found frozen in a glacier in the Alps a few years back? He's got only 11 pairs of ribs. It happens. Still, imagine what might happen if the creation scientists get a hold of a replica of the 5,300-year-old-man skeleton and try to pawn it off as proof of the Bible" (Root-Bernstein, 1995).

Yes, imagine if this body does hold a biblical secret. Some of the world's greatest scientists, for example, Isaac Newton, were brilliant enough to understand how God and science are connected. Many schools fail to teach that Newton was a devout Christian and spent most of his life studying the Bible. In Newton, we find a man of true faith and great wisdom.

Once more, the body of the Iceman yields a secret and gives one more piece of fascinating information. The body of the Iceman can be read like a book. Every aspect of the life of Cain somehow is embedded in this incredible frozen man—a man sealed away like a human time capsule for a future generation to decipher. Are we approaching a point in our investigation where a logical verdict can be reached?

Chapter 8

The Curse

O F ALL THE evidence we have discussed up to this point, there is none more fascinating and complex than the curse. In fact, this aspect of the study almost kept me from writing the book altogether. I could hardly wrap my mind around all the possibilities of what this could mean without my emotions overtaking me. But to exclude it altogether would be a glaring omission in the Bible's testimony about Cain. It also is so obvious that it would have been seen as a huge oversight and generated misinformation. The truth of the matter is that the story of Cain tells of a sevenfold curse. The story of the Iceman tells of a curse that affected seven people. I am simply putting two and two together and saying, "Judge the evidence for yourself."

In my younger years, I considered a curse to be a myth or

superstition having no relevance in everyday life. As a Christian, I believe we are protected from curses and that God has given us a sound mind rather than a spirit of fear, but there are certain curses God has manifested that do affect us. I had to ask myself, "What is different about this curse that would make me believe it is not just hype? Is there logic and truth to back up the assumption that there is a curse of the Iceman? And, could the curse of Otzi actually be the sevenfold curse of Cain?"

I began to look at curses in the Bible. As stated earlier, Adam and Eve were forced to leave the garden, and God cursed the ground so it would be difficult to grow food. Man would live by the sweat of his brow. As a general rule of life, man has always had to work to survive. And, as far as plants are concerned, it takes a lot of work and planning to grow food, whereas weeds will grow everywhere. Here is a curse that was made approximately 6,000 years ago, and we still are living with its effects today. At the same time, God also cursed Eve so that childbearing would be difficult and painful. Any woman who has given birth can tell you how true this is! Even with all the drugs and medical advancements, childbirth and the recovery is still extremely painful.

In the Old Testament, God warned Israel that if the people turned away from him, he would curse them from their land and disperse them all around the world. He also said that when they turned back to him, he would bring them back to Israel and heal their land. History tells us how the Jews were dispersed around the world until the events of World War II. And, we saw the miracle of God returning them to their land in the Middle

East when Israel became a nation against all odds in 1948. We see this curse on Israel coming to completion within the past century, still having relevance thousands of years later.

God's biblical curses are true, logical, and relevant in modern society. We see proof of them every day. We are all affected by them regardless of whether we admit it or not. The curse God put on Cain is no different. God's righteous judgment brought these curses into existence, and even thousands of years later they remain valid.

The curse of Cain is difficult to describe, because if you read through the ancient manuscripts, there is more than a single application. Probably the easiest way to comprehend this curse is to think of it as having many different layers that are interwoven. The curse affected not only Cain but also his descendants. *The Antiquities of the Jews* says, "God therefore did not inflict the punishment of death upon him, on account of his offering sacrifice, and thereby making supplication to him not to be extreme in His wrath to him; but He made him accursed, and threatened his posterity in the seventh generation" (Whiston, 1987). We have read how Cain's lifestyle and bad choices affected all of his children and their children, each becoming more wicked.

Another layer certainly applied to those who killed Cain, Lamech and Tubal (who were the seventh generation). If we read the original Hebrew translation of the Bible, it also appears to affect those finding his body. In the book of Jude, we see yet another layer falling on the people who have "gone the way of Cain" in the latter days; these people will be destroyed. These layers can be seen in the effects on specific people and on whole groups of people.

The curse God placed on Cain impacted his life in several ways. First, Cain was cursed to wander with all those who belonged to him, living in fear with no permanent home.

Second, he was cursed from the ground. This meant he could not grow his own food anymore, and it also meant he would not be buried in the ground like his brother Abel.

Third, he was to be hidden from the face of God. This had both spiritual and physical fulfillments, meaning he would not be able to have a relationship with God and would be hidden away from him (perhaps in an icy tomb).

Fourth, Cain was marked physically as a sign to warn others of his murderous nature. I believe the markings of *vav vav vav,* or *666,* were meant so that anyone finding him could recognize the specific number of this man, be it 3300 BC or AD 1991.

The next, or fifth, layer of the curse fell on people who came into contact with Cain. The curse would fall on those involved in the finding and smiting of Cain, and this in itself would be a sevenfold curse.

The sixth layer was Cain's enslavement to Satan, who became his master. He became the original son of perdition and altered a world where people once lived generously and peacefully among each other.

And last, there is the righteous-judgment portion of the curse where Cain killed Abel with a stone, so with a stone he was killed in righteous judgment. The righteous-judgment portion of the curse goes out to all people past and present and is said to be written in the heavenly tablets. This portion basically says that a person who murders his neighbor is cursed, and anyone who sees it and does not declare it shall be cursed like Cain.

Cain makes an interesting statement in response to the curses God put upon him. Genesis says Cain said, "and it shall come to pass, that every one that findeth me shall smite me." Cain was speaking of what was to come in the future. Why would Cain make this statement—that everyone who finds him will smite him—when a man can be killed only once? Suppose we made this statement come out of the mouth of Otzi. How ironic, yet so true, that everyone who finds him, or studies him, wants to dissect him, probe him, cut him open, look at his insides, and remove parts of his body; it probably will be this way until the end of mankind. This might not be what Cain had in mind, but it does seem fitting in a bizarre sort of way.

Many magazine and news reports have speculated that there might be a curse surrounding the Iceman. If you do a little research on the subject, you will find numerous articles about the seven people who have died from this "curse." An extensive book was published in French pertaining to the mummy curse and these seven people (Benhamou & Sabroux, 2006). Most media reports try to write the curse off as sensationalist hype, or suggest that it is just a crude attempt to revive the same hoopla the "curse of King Tut" caused back in 1922. Even so, it has not diminished the suspicion that there is indeed some kind of curse hanging over the Iceman.

The inescapable fact is that seven people directly involved

with the discovery and research of the Iceman have died traumatically or became terminally ill and died after involvement with the mummy. Only one, Dieter Warnecke, did not work directly with the Iceman's body, but the circumstances of his death add a strange twist that only deepens the mystery.

The following is a list of the victims of the "curse."

1. The first victim was Dr. Rainer Henn, sixty-four, who was the head of the forensic team that helped to retrieve and make the first official examination of the body. Henn died in a head-on collision in 1992 while on his way to a conference where he was to speak about the Iceman.

2. The second victim was mountaineer Kurt Fritz, fifty-two, who led the team that retrieved the Iceman's body from the mountain. He and Dr. Henn actually pulled the body from the ice. In 1992, shortly after Henn's death, Fritz was the only member of his mountain-climbing party to be struck and killed in an avalanche.

3. The third victim was journalist Rainer Hoelzl, forty-seven. He exclusively covered the removal of the body from the mountain as part of a one-hour documentary that was shown around the world. He died of a brain tumor a few months after Kurt Fritz's death.

4. The fourth victim was mountain climber Helmut Simon, sixty-seven, the man who actually found the Iceman's body. Although some papers have referred to Simon as the "father of Otzi," he seemed to have considered

himself the "brother of Otzi," according to one reporter from *The Guardian*. Several times each year, he and his wife, Erika, visited Bolzano, where the Iceman is exhibited. As his discoverer, he developed a kind of brotherly connection to Otzi and referred to him as his "brother."

In 2004, Mr. Simon went climbing in the same mountain range where he had found the Iceman. He was celebrating the large monetary award he had just won in court for finding the body when he fell down a 300-foot cliff during a freak blizzard. Dieter Warnecke, head of the rescue team that found Simon's body, said he was found in the exact same position as the Iceman, lying on his stomach with his left arm straight across under his chin.

5. The fifth victim was Dieter Warnecke, forty-five, the head of the mountain-rescue team that recovered Helmut Simon's body. He died of a sudden heart attack the same hour Helmut Simon was buried. His only link to the Iceman was finding Mr. Simon's body.

6. The sixth victim was archaeologist Konrad Spindler, fifty-five, the leading expert on the 5,300-year-old corpse. Dr. Spindler was the first archaeologist to examine Otzi and realize how extremely old the body was. He thought that finding Otzi was just as incredible as the discovery of King Tut. Spindler died from complications related to multiple sclerosis.

7. The seventh victim was Dr. Tom Loy, sixty-three, who died before finishing his extensive book on the Iceman. He was the head of the DNA research team. Dr. Loy died in 2005 but was diagnosed with thrombophilia, a rare blood-clotting disease, shortly after he began research on the Iceman. He died after twelve years of battling this disease.

As an indication of how the story of the curse had gotten "legs," the BBC released this news report shortly after Dr. Loy's death: "Death Renews Iceman 'Curse' Claim: Should Working with Otzi Carry a Health Warning?"

> The death of a molecular biologist has fuelled renewed speculation about a "curse" connected to an ancient corpse. Tom Loy, 63, had analyzed DNA found on "Otzi," the Stone Age hunter whose remains were discovered in 1991. Dr. Loy died in unclear circumstances in Australia two weeks ago; it has been announced, making him the seventh person connected with Otzi to die. Colleagues and family of Dr Loy have rejected the notion that he was the victim of a "curse." It is not known how many people have worked on the Otzi project—and whether the death rate is statistically high. ("Death Renews Iceman 'Curse' Claim," 2005)

Let's try to put these bizarre events into perspective. Here is a comparison with another group of seven individuals who were the first Americans to venture into space:

On Sunday, February 24, 2002, the six surviving members of the original seven Mercury astronauts celebrated forty years of American space flight at the Kennedy Space Center. Four of the original astronauts were in attendance, another two had other commitments but still sent their regards, and only Gus Grisom, who had died, could not be involved in the celebration. Here we have a similar group of seven people, working in a hazardous profession, and over a period of forty years we have only one death. Compare this with the seven people working in close contact with the Iceman over a period of fourteen years.

By comparison, the curse of the Iceman would be equivalent to all seven of the original Mercury astronauts dying tragic deaths during the first fourteen years of the space program. I have read comments from supposedly knowledgeable people who say statistically there is nothing abnormal about these deaths, but I cannot agree with that assessment; there definitely is something out of the ordinary going on here.

It would not be surprising for a few of the many people involved in discovery and research of the Iceman to die within a few years after working with the mummy; however, it is quite surprising that the seven men who have died were at the very center of the Iceman story. These individuals were directly involved in the events related to the findings of the Iceman. Note, too, that all of these men died at relatively young ages; the oldest was only sixty-seven, and two were in their forties.

The seven men who died were not just bystanders; these

were the main players. Look at the lineup: the man who found the body, the man who took the body off the mountain, the first doctor to examine the body, the man who documented the body's discovery, the scientist who performed all the DNA research, the leading authority in the study of the body, and finally the man who recovered the body of the Iceman's discoverer. Seven is a significant number in Scripture because it denotes completion and finality.

The common denominator among this small group of people is the simple fact that their lives converged at an incident we call "the finding of the Iceman." With this in mind, read the exact wording of the curse of Cain found in the Bible.

Here is the original Hebrew text where it gives the sevenfold curse of Cain, from Genesis 4:15 in the Hebrew Interlinear Bible:

> u-iamr l-u ieue lkn kl erg qin shbothim iqm
>
> and-he-is-saying to-him, Yahweh, therefore every-of one-killing of-Cain sevenfold he-shall-be-avenged.
>
> u-ishm ieue l-qin auth l-blthi ekuth ath-u kl mtza-u
>
> And-he-is-placing, Yahweh, on-Cain (a) sign to-so-as-not to-smite of-him every-of one-finding-of-him.

Read it again, "finding of him." And that is where the verse stops!

Statistically, if this were the body of Cain, the curse indicates that seven would die, and this would complete the curse. But it is not until we study the way in which these men died that we begin to see the full circle of what could be the curse taking place. In order to do this, we have to go back to Cain and how he murdered his own brother.

Cain killed his brother with a stone, the head of his tilling tool, which looked similar to an ax. Most would think a metal ax is not a rock, but actually it is, and it would have been considered a rock back in that day. The ax would have been formed by taking several stones containing copper ore and heating them in a fire at approximately 2,000 degrees Fahrenheit. At this temperature, the copper would begin to melt and separate. Later, the copper, or melted rock, would have been heated again and remolded into a cast so that when it hardened, it would form the shape of an ax. Thus, Abel was murdered with a stone.

The Book of Jubilees says, "For with a stone he had killed Abel, and by a stone was he (Cain) killed in righteous judgment." Here we see that because Cain killed Abel, his own family, with a stone, he likewise was killed by his own family with a stone, an arrowhead. After Tubal and Lamech found and killed Cain, we see how the righteous-judgment curse was passed to them. The next person to suffer from the curse was Tubal, who directed his father to kill Cain by raising his hands so his father would shoot the arrow. Immediately afterward, they discovered it was Cain they had killed and not an animal. Lamech became enraged. Tubal then was killed in the same way he had been involved in killing Cain—by the hands of his father, Lamech. The righteous judgment next was passed on to Lamech, who said that because he killed Cain, he would be cursed. It was not the sevenfold curse, however, because the righteous-judgment portion of the curse caused it to be much more severe. The curse that affected Lamech and his children was a seventy-seven-fold curse as recorded in the Bible.

We thus begin to see a pattern that I call the righteous-judgment pattern of those who incur the curse of Cain. It begins with Cain dying in the same way he killed Abel and then branches out to those who were involved in the finding and smiting of Cain. *The Book of Jubilees* says the following:

> The Lord blamed Cain, because he killed Abel, and He made him a fugitive on the earth because of the blood of his brother, and He cursed him on the earth. Because of this it is written on the heavenly tablets, "Cursed is he who kills his neighbor treacherously, and let all who have seen and heard say, 'So be it,' and the man who has seen and not reported it, let him be accursed as the one committing it." (Lumpkin, 2006)

Now, I want to say first that I do not believe these men deserved to die for anything they did or did not do. Since the death of Christ, we live in the age of grace. I am not a judge of others. I have sinned just as much as anyone else and I know I deserve to be punished. That is why I cling to Jesus, my Savior, who took my punishment. My heart goes out to the families of these great men. But I cannot overlook the way this pattern falls into place. It appears that each person who died in relation to the Iceman's curse died in a way that reflects how he interacted with Otzi's body. I have noticed this peculiar twist, which seems to lend credibility to the sevenfold curse attached to the finding of Cain. Let's examine the scenarios surrounding the "victims of Otzi's curse."

1. The first victim was Dr. Rainer Henn, the head of the forensic team. With the help of Kurt Fritz, he retrieved the body and was the first person to have the body transported to Innsbruck, where he made the first official examination of the body. A year later, he became the first victim of the curse. While driving himself to speak at a conference about the Iceman, he died in a head-on collision. The first person to transport the Iceman becomes the first person to die in an automobile accident.

2. The second victim was mountaineer Kurt Fritz, the head of the team that retrieved the Iceman's body from the ice. He was the one who actually pulled the body of the Iceman out of the mountain, with the help of Dr. Henn. The following year, shortly after Henn's death, Fritz was buried in an avalanche. He was the only person in his mountain-climbing party to be struck. The person who

pulled Otzi out of his icy grave dies by being covered in an icy grave.

3. Next is journalist Rainer Hoelzl, who showed up on the mountaintop to document and record the removal of the body, so that an account would be preserved. He filmed a one-hour documentary that was shown around the world, sending out the communication of the discovery of the Iceman. Hoelzl died of a brain tumor a few months after Kurt Fritz's death. This connection is difficult to make with the current information available. What I do see is that Hoelzl's brain, the part of his body that documented, recorded, and preserved images, was destroyed, thus taking his life. His work sent out the message of Otzi's discovery around the world. Shortly after, his brain's ability to send out messages to his body was taken.

4. The fourth victim was mountain climber Helmut Simon. This is where things begin to get eerie. Simon and his wife found Otzi in the Alps when they were climbing. Simon visited Otzi's body several times each year at the museum and called him a "brother." Thirteen years after the discovery of the Iceman, Simon finally won a court case that entitled him to a finder's fee for Otzi. To celebrate, Simon climbed into the Otzal mountains. A freak blizzard blew in, making it difficult for him to hike. He fell down a 300-foot cliff and died. When the head of the rescue team found Simon, he said the position

they found him in was unusual. Simon was frozen dead in the same position in which Otzi had been found, lying on his stomach with his left arm straight underneath his chin. It was almost as though he had taken Otzi's place. The man who first discovered the Iceman while climbing dies climbing and is found frozen in ice, laying in the exact same position the mummy was found.

5. The fifth victim, Dieter Warnecke, never interacted with the body of the Iceman. He was the head of the mountain-rescue team that found Helmut Simon's deceased body in the peculiar position mimicking the Iceman. His only connection to the Iceman was recovering Simon, the man who discovered Otzi. The peculiar thing about his death is that he died of a heart attack the very hour Helmut Simon was buried. He was in his forties, and his family said he had been in perfect health. To reiterate, Warnecke discovers the body of the Iceman's discoverer, who mimicked the death of Otzi. The very same hour Simon is being buried in the earth; Warnecke has a massive heart attack and dies. His death was connected to the death and burial of Simon, his only connection to the mummy.

6. Konrad Spindler, a highly acclaimed archaeologist, became the sixth victim after mocking the claim of a curse. He was the leading expert and author on the 5,300-year-old corpse. It was Spindler who was called in by Dr. Rainer Henn to examine the Iceman shortly after the mummy was recovered. Dr. Spindler was the

first person to realize how extremely old the body was and actually saved it. Dr. Spindler noticed when he first examined the mummy that a fungus was growing all over it. He was the first archaeologist to put a protective covering all over the mummy, hence saving it from rapid deterioration. Dr. Spindler dismissed the link between the five previous victims, declaring, "I suppose you will be saying I am the next to die." Little did he know he would be the next! Not long after Spindler made this statement, he died from complications related to multiple sclerosis, a disease that destroys the protective covering of the nervous system and causes the body to deteriorate rapidly. The man in charge of protecting, covering, and preventing destruction of Otzi's tissue died when the protective covering of his nervous system deteriorated and was destroyed.

7. The seventh victim was a man I consider an absolute expert. Dr. Tom Loy was a DNA specialist who studied the microscopic remains of blood on ancient artifacts. He died before finishing his book on his studies of the Iceman. Dr. Loy was the head of the DNA research team. He died of a rare blood disease he had been battling since the time he had come in contact with the Iceman. In another peculiar twist, the head scientist who studied the blood found on and around the Iceman dies of a rare blood disease.

Could these incidences really be part of the curse of Cain?

To tell you the truth, I don't know. But these stories are so uncanny that they seem to be supernatural. And I cannot help but think that this body really could be the body of Cain. Was God being literal when he said there would be a sevenfold curse for the finding and smiting of Cain? A curse from God Almighty is fearsome and not to be ignored or taken lightly.

I keep asking myself why God would place a curse on Cain that would result in the death of seven other people. Would God be willing to take the lives of seven of his children to exact some kind of revenge for the death of one murderous liar? I cannot imagine God doing that. I can only think that God was just stating the fact that when Cain was found, seven of the people involved in the finding would die. He told us so we would know, and that is why he said he was making Cain a sign.

Everyone on this earth is destined to die. Eventually every person who has worked on the Iceman will pass away through the course of time. These incredible men died at their appointed time. Their paths just crossed the path of the Iceman and, in turn, they became a part of something greater, something bigger than us.

As Christians, we believe they are precious to God, and their lives likewise are precious to us. God views death entirely differently from how we do. For him, it is the passageway into everlasting life, for every man is appointed once to die. There is an appointed time for everything, a time to live and a time to die, and all of our days are already numbered. The very God who gives us our spirit and body here on the earth will put our body to "sleep," and our soul will go on to live for eternity either with God or separated from him.

I do not believe the destinies of these seven people were altered or their lives were cut short by their encounter with Otzi. I believe they lived their lives fulfilling their destiny. When their appointment with death arrived, they completed the plan for their lives. I think their destinies all crossed a common point when they came into contact with the Iceman. I think all this happened so we would know that the Iceman could be Cain, and that the world is rushing headlong toward the way of Cain.

Chapter 9

The Sign

As I said at the beginning, in God's economy, nothing happens by accident. The very existence of this body approaches the definition of miraculous even by secular standards. Regardless of your belief or unbelief in God, however, judging strictly from a standpoint of logic, the scientific evidence and the ancient historical records support the hypothesis that this could be the body of Cain.

The circumstantial evidence, if viewed by a forensic pathologist, could be credible enough to identify any modern-day John Doe. If this were a case of a missing person and a detective knew the time of death, the cause of death, and had an identifying mark such as a tattoo, he or she would be able to make a positive identification. Is the evidence on the Iceman enough to convince the average person with an open mind?

Well, I can speak only for myself; in that, I am quite amazed by the volume of evidence collected from the body of a man more than 5,000 years old.

If this is, in fact, the body of Cain, I would have to commend almost every scientist mentioned in this book for their research. How incredible to describe this man as a wanderer and determine that he was killed by an arrowhead by his own kinsmen. And how valuable is this relic that the Museum of South Tyrol owns? Of course the data will never be 100 percent conclusive, but I am persuaded to believe this really could be the body of Cain. The Iceman cannot stand up and say, "Hey! I'm Cain!" But many unique features of this body seems to say it is.

The crux of the matter comes down to this: The Iceman was preserved for all these thousands of years either by happenstance or as the result of a supernatural intervention. That intervention would be to reveal something important. If you are inclined to think this is the body of Cain, then there is something more we should consider.

The Bible says God marked Cain as a "sign." So, what is a sign? The Hebrew word for a sign is *oth,* and this is what it means:

Strong's concordance Hebrew: 226. אות (oth) –

a mark, miracle, ensign, (in the sense of appearing); a signal

(literally or figuratively), as a flag, beacon,

monument, omen, prodigy, evidence, etc. (Biblos. com, n.d.)

If the Iceman's body is the body of Cain, it definitely would fit the description of a miracle. Certainly, his body showing up after all these years would qualify as a wonder, giving evidence in the sense of an appearing. The marking of Cain's body also was meant to be an omen, or a warning.

A few things become evident when we acknowledge the connection between the Iceman and Cain. First, this discovery could provide indisputable proof of the accuracy of Genesis. Second, understanding the turpitude of Cain's evil nature would clarify the warning in Jude's epistle telling us that many would follow the way of Cain, and further study of the Scripture sets the time period in an era referred to as the end of the age. Third, if Cain's body conveys a warning, it would be imperative to find out exactly what it is. And finally, we would have to decide either to heed the warning or ignore it. Jude 1:11, King James Version, says, "Woe unto them! For they have gone in the way of Cain, and ran greedily after the error of Balaam for reward, and perished in the gainsaying of Core."

Ironically, the number of the Scripture is *111,* making the same marking as *vav vav vav,* like that found on the Iceman. *The error of Balaam* in broad terms means "selfishness, greed, fornication, idolatry, and false teaching." *The gainsaying of Core* pertains to rebellion, strife, deception, and disregarding authority. When we read the book of Jude, we are warned that the apostasy of the church will be happening at the same time the depravity of the world increases. We see this also in 2 Timothy 3:1–5, where we read the following:

> But know this, that in the last days perilous times will come: For men will be lovers of themselves, lovers of money, boasters, proud, blasphemers, disobedient to parents, unthankful, unholy, unloving, unforgiving, slanderers, without self-control, brutal, despisers of good, traitors, headstrong, haughty, lovers of pleasure rather than lovers of God, having a form of godliness but denying its power. And from such people turn away!

This describes a world where the vast majority of people have the same characteristics as Cain. We would do well to heed this warning, because deception works only when the victim believes a lie and rejects the truth.

Most people perceive time moving in a long, straight line, but some see time as a great circle, repeating events over and over with different people and places. There appears to be a great circle of time in the Bible. That is to say, if we want to discern Revelation, we find it necessary to look back to Genesis. Jesus himself said, "As it was in the days of Noah so shall it be at the coming of the Son of Man." If we want to comprehend how things will be at the end of this present age, we need to understand how events will complete the account that started way back in Genesis.

I want to be cautious about where we are in God's plan for mankind. The Bible is clear that no man knows the day or the hour when the end of this age will be. It could be this year or it could be a thousand years from now. Furthermore, the Bible also is clear that the end of the age is not the end of the world, as many people have assumed. After the destruction caused by the tribulation period, the earth will be restored and go on for another thousand years at least.

Jesus gave us many signs to watch for so we can recognize the end of the age. Many biblical scholars and pastors believe several of these signs are coming to pass. Either way, we should always be ready in our hearts for the return of the Lord, because you never know what day you will meet your maker.

Although we are currently experiencing some of the most horrific natural disasters in history, we also have witnessed incredible archaeological discoveries since the rebirth of modern-day Israel. These include finding the Dead Sea Scrolls, the potential discovery of Noah's ark in Iran, the three-dimensional images produced within the Shroud of Turin, the astronomical discovery of the star of Bethlehem, the body of the Iceman, and much more. Could it be true that by the end, there will be no more mysteries, no more gaps, and God will have answered all the questions? Mark 4:22, New King James Version, says, "For there is nothing hidden which will not be revealed, nor has anything been kept secret but that it should come to light."

In my opinion, the evidence that the Iceman's body is the body of Cain goes beyond happenstance and coincidence. The markings are a potent witness and powerful warning. Could

Cain's curse be an active force at work in the world today? Knowledge has increased dramatically in the last 200 years, and through the sciences of archaeology, archaeo-astronomy, and the decoding of ancient languages, much of the biblical text can now be verified scientifically. In the Bible, God was marking Cain for a sign. To understand what the sign is, we need to look at the marks found on the Iceman and figure out how they might apply to our present age.

One of these great scientific discoveries occurred in 1905 when Sir William Flinders Petrie found inscriptions at Serabit el-Khadim in the Sinai Peninsula that became known as Proto-Sinaitic script (Petrie, 1906). As more of these inscriptions were found, it was announced that this script was the oldest written language and the origin of all alphabetical languages in the world.

In chapter 4 we interpreted the markings found on Otzi's body to be the ancient Hebrew Proto-Sinaitic letters *tav (X)*, *vav (I)*, and *lamed (C)*, embedded deep in his skin. We deciphered the numeric value of the *III* marks as the number *666*, which is the mark of the beast found in Revelation 13. In addition, we deciphered *tav (X)* as the ancient Hebrew letter or symbol for a mark and a sign. Looking deeper, we found on Otzi's wrist the *C* mark, which means "to control" and suggests the action of piercing the skin. In the ancient accounts, we read that Cain became the first person to deteriorate into the spiritual condition we call a reprobate mind. For this, God made him bear a mark to indicate that his master was Satan.

Is it possible a mark similar to Cain's mark will be placed on those who worship the beast during the time of great tribulation? The mark of the beast may appear as a small *X* or three short lines, |||. It could even be placed under the skin, making it invisible other than a small scar.

Here is the passage in Revelation 13:17–18 (KJV) telling us about the mark of the beast:

> And that no man might buy or sell, save he that had the mark, or the name of the beast, or the number of his name. Here is wisdom. Let him that hath understanding count the number of the beast: for it is the number of a man; and his number is Six hundred threescore and six.

Interestingly, the Bible says that this mark corresponds to the name of the beast and the number of his name. We know the Antichrist will be a real person empowered and ultimately possessed by Satan, but why does the Scripture indicate that the mark he will force everyone to take contains the number *666* and the name of the beast? The beast is also referred to as Leviathan in the Old Testament, but where do we find a man with the number *666*?

The Bible says to let him that has understanding count, or explain, the number of the beast, for it is the number of a man. Could it be a man mentioned in the Bible who would be familiar to almost everyone in the world? A man who was known for bringing evil practices into the world? A man who is the archetype of the reprobate human condition at the end of the age? These verses have mystified scholars for centuries, but I would like to present some tantalizing new information that may lead to an answer.

Following is a drawing of the fragment of the Oxyrhynchus Papyri, or P-115, found in Egypt in 1895. This is a fragment of the oldest existing copy of the book of Revelation. It dates from the mid- to late third century, approximately AD 225–275. The mark of the beast is shown on the third line of the fragment.

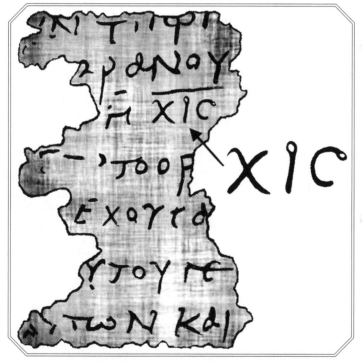

© Drawing of the Oxyrhynchus Papyri, or P-115. Artwork by O. Thomas

If these three symbols (X, I, C) are interpreted as Proto-Sinaitic Hebrew letters, we find a remarkable meaning. Compare the Papyri symbols to the Proto-Sinaitic letters *tav X, vav I,* and *lamed C.*

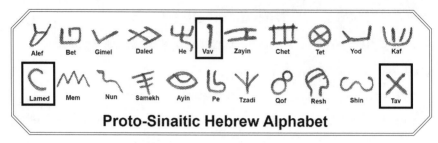

© XIC found in the ancient alphabet. Artwork by O. Thomas

Could it be possible that these symbols on the P-115 Papyri are not Greek letters at all, but relic symbols from a more remote time? The symbols on the P-115 fragment interpreted in the ancient Hebrew reveal what the mark of the beast may look like. These letters may spell out the actual name of the beast because the word they produce "Levitaw" is the primitive root for the name Leviathan mentioned in the Bible. These symbols may have been passed down from the time of Adam, because two of the symbols, *X* and *I,* were considered to be the marks engraved on Cain.

In this ancient Hebrew alphabet, *C* is the letter *lamed,* which means "to direct or control," as in giving instructions (Ancient Hebrew Research Center, 1999). The letter is a pictogram of a goad used to prod cattle. A goad was a staff with a sharp spike on one end. *Lamed* also has a verb form meaning "to puncture or pierce the skin." The only man ever mentioned in the Bible to be marked was Cain; he is the personification of the proverbial marked man. The marks on Cain were a warning of his curse and would have been recorded and passed down from one generation to another.

To reiterate, the symbol *X* is *tav,* meaning "a mark and a sign." The symbol *I* is *vav,* a pictogram of a peg; it means "to attach like a nail, or to hook into like a fish." *Vav* has a numeric value of 6, the number of man. The symbol *C* is *lamed,* meaning "to direct or control," as in giving instructions, and as a verb meaning "to pierce the skin." This is the symbolic meaning of the three symbols when added together:

Marked for a sign—with a nail or peg hooked into like a fishhook—that will be used to control and direct.

I was flabbergasted when I realized what this 1,800-year-old papyrus was describing: being marked with a peg attached to you that controls and directs. This immediately made me think of a radio-frequency identification device (RFID) that is available in tattoo ink. However, it wouldn't have to be that sophisticated if people willingly accepted a mark showing their allegiance to the beast.

We are moving into a world ruled by logistics where everyone is a number. Tracking and identifying people has become the focus of industry, medicine, banking, and governments. In the name of safety, governments become our masters. We can see that systems are being set into place throughout the world, where it will be possible to have global banking and governance.

The technology to implement the mark of the beast exists today, whereas ten years ago, people still were questioning how it could be possible. Many countries around the world are already using forms of RFID in their national ID cards. Implementing RFID tattoos would simply be the next step in making complete control of the individual inescapable.

No one can say exactly how or when the mark-of-the-beast

system would be used on a global scale, but even now, world economies are so fragile that it would take only one major calamity to start a worldwide panic. Most people would rush to any system offering security and promising the necessities of life. Though we do not know when the events of Revelation will take place, we do know the technology is available.

The conditions of the world we live in compel me to ask you this question: Is the reality of the world we live in just the product of perpetual chaos, or is our reality the result of a grand scheme, unfolding with reason and purpose? Our world paradigm is viewed as having either order or chaos, depending on our belief in either divine or random creation.

To be honest, a person's paradigm—their reality—is the result of their own choices. Needless to say, choose wisely. Search for the Lord with all your heart. The road is narrow, and one path leads to oblivion, whereas the other path leads to divine providence.

Chapter 10

The Verdict

OULD THE BODY of Otzi the Iceman actually be the body of Cain? For the first time in history, we can ask this implausible question, because likewise, for the first time in history, we have a highly preserved body dating to this ancient era. Finding the body of a man who, according to biblical chronology, lived when Adam was still alive raises this question: Who was this man?

I would like to start this chapter by summarizing the circumstantial evidence provided in this book and adding some interesting facts. The Iceman's time of death is estimated by carbon dating to be approximately 3092 BC. By comparison, Cain's estimated time of death is about 3074 BC, using Ussher's biblical chronology. The exact date of death is unattainable, but the most important fact remains: these two men lived in the same era and could have died at the exact same time. The difference of eighteen years between the death of Otzi and the death of Cain is a reasonable match. By historical standards, Otzi and Cain died at approximately the same time.

One big obstacle for those who reject the notion of ancient people's extreme longevity is the difference between the estimated age of Otzi and that of Cain. Scientists estimate Otzi's age to have been approximately forty-five years, whereas ancient historical records indicate that Cain lived more than 800 years. Having no precise method for determining Otzi's age scientists compared his arthritic bone condition to that of typical modern humans and arrived at an estimated age of forty-five years. This method seems reasonable at first, but this is meaningless if people lived longer, healthier lives in the distant past.

Extreme longevity in ancient records is not unusual. For example, in ancient Chinese history we find a legendary man named Peng Zu who was believed to have lived for more than 800 years during the Yin dynasty (sixteenth to eleventh centuries BC). Additionally, there is a Greek record dating from the second century AD of a person called the Blind Seer of Thebes, who is said to have lived six generations, which would be close to 300 years. These are just two cases from literally hundreds of reports of ancient people living long lives. We have no examples of 800-year-old people to compare Otzi with, so how do we prove that his body is not that of a man more than 800 years old?

One of Otzi's interesting physical anomalies could have been the result of his extreme age. His teeth were as flat as a rail, both in shape and in alignment (Murphy Jr. et al., 2003). The teeth were ground perfectly flat, to the point that he had no distinguishable canine teeth. Flat teeth would be one attribute we would expect to see in an extremely old body.

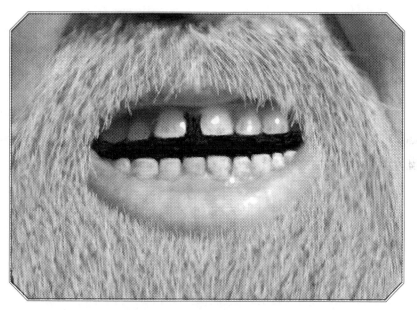

© Example of Iceman's teeth, showing extreme bruxism. Artwork by O. Thomas

For this condition to be present in a forty-five-year-old man would indicate that sand must have been the mainstay of his diet. We know, however, that Otzi was a hunter, and that meat was the core of his diet. Would eating meat for forty-five years cause one's teeth to become completely flat? Needless to say, the flat-tooth anomaly is still a serious point of debate among Otzi researchers. Guessing his age to be forty-five is still a guess, and is just as inconclusive as saying he was 861 years old.

Finding that both Otzi and Cain died from an arrow

wound is astounding. Most murder cases dating back more than ten years become cold cases and are rarely solved. In the mysterious case of the murdered Iceman, we might have the outlandish good fortune of a full confession from Otzi's killer. *The Ancient Book of Jasher* tells us the circumstances, the murder weapon, and the name of the perpetrator, all in graphic detail. The cause of death for both Otzi and Cain was an arrow shot from a great distance by a member of his own clan. Both men died almost instantly from the massive internal injury and fell dead in their tracks. Both men were killed in the wilderness. Both men were dressed in a way that they could have passed for an animal.

Based on *The Ancient Book of Jasher,* we can make the allegation that Lamech killed Otzi. We will not call this a murder, because, as we determined earlier, it was a case of involuntary manslaughter during a hunting accident. The 5,300-year-old murder case now has a realistic explanation. Otzi and Cain both suffered their demise after a fatal arrow wound.

Rabbinic scholars using the *Zohar* and other ancient records concluded the mark on Cain was the letter *vav.* Otzi's body also has the letter *vav* engraved on it. The ancient Hebrew letter *vav* looks like the letter *I* and has a numeric value of 6. Symbolically *vav* means to affix or set. The Bible says God set a mark on Cain for a sign. The ancient Hebrew letter that means "a mark" and "a sign" is the letter *tav* written as *X.* The letter *X* also is engraved on Otzi's body. These two permanent and unique markings are sufficient to identify Cain, and the fact that we find these markings on Otzi leads to an obvious conclusion: Otzi and Cain have the same identifying marks on their bodies.

The DNA evidence is consistent with a man who died before the flood and matches unique traits we would expect of Cain. Otzi's DNA is so unique that he has his own classification representing an entire branch of the human race that has vanished from the face of the earth. Although it is believed that he has distant relatives alive today, none are from his direct line.

Additional DNA evidence found on his body indicates that he was of a violent nature, having the blood of three other people on his weapons. Otzi's DNA carried a mutation causing him to have only eleven sets of ribs instead of the normal twelve ribs on each side. The DNA evidence pertaining to Otzi and the ancient historical information found about Cain indicate that both Otzi and Cain died before the great flood, and that any descendants they had died in the flood.

There is microscopic evidence in the form of a unique giant bacterium discovered in Otzi's body that came from a species of fish found only in the Red Sea. This indicates that Otzi walked great distances during his life and traveled to the area of the Red Sea shortly before he died. This parallels the account given in *The Book of Jubilees* saying that shortly before Cain died, he traveled to the area we now call Israel, near the Red Sea, for the funeral of his father. Otzi and Cain both traveled great distances, were identified as wanderers, and were most likely in an area near the Red Sea shortly before they died.

All of the critical circumstances that preserved the Iceman's body came about with perfect timing and sequence. What are the odds that a person would die while falling into a protective trench and then become completely freeze-dried?

I doubt anyone would have realized the significance of that portion of Cain's curse saying he never would be buried until the discovery of Otzi and his similarities to Cain. There are several other mysterious correlations between these two men. Here are some additional interesting connections:

> » The Iceman's body was encased in ice and hidden for fifty centuries. He was found positioned facedown with his arm in front of him. He almost looked as though he was hiding. Cain said his punishment was more than he could bear and that from God's face he should be hid.

> » The Iceman's body was encased in a massive glacier that slowly melted, bringing his body to the surface and exposing it. Cain's curse included the statement that he would be driven out of the face of the earth.

> » The Iceman's body is preserved in a high-tech, computerized, refrigeration unit and will never decompose. It is far too valuable a discovery to be given a proper burial. Cain's body was cursed from the ground that opened up to receive Abel's body, implying he would never be buried in the ground.

> » The Iceman is the oldest human body ever found. Cain

is the first human being ever born, making his body the oldest human born on earth.

» The Iceman is from the haplogroup K-1. There is a K-1 haplogroup identified in modern society, but no people who would be direct descendants of Otzi.

» The Iceman has numerous markings on his body. Cain is the only man specifically mentioned in the Bible to be marked on his body. The Iceman's tattoos are not typical needle-and-ink tattoos. Incisions were made into the skin and filled with a substance believed to be soot, which contained precious stones. The pigment created black and blue scars. These are not self-inflicted; many are on his back. Cain's markings were not typical, because they were made by God himself. Cain was marked after he made a burnt offering to God. Many people believe that anything that God touches will turn to precious stones.

» The Iceman's body has symbols on it from the Proto-Sinaitic alphabet. This is the original Hebrew alphabet. It is also the oldest alphabet and the origin of all written languages. According to Hebrew tradition, this written language was used before the Tower of Babel and goes back to the time of Adam and Cain.

» The X and I are now used as a symbol for the Iceman. There is a new line of Otzi shoes for sale. The logo is an X and an I. The logo used at the museum where Otzi is kept has a picture of him standing next to a giant letter *X*. Historically, the *X* has been used as the symbol for Cain by different people, tribes, and cultures. Many of the petroglyphs found in the area of Val Senales, where the Iceman lived, depict a fierce individual with an *X* prominently placed on his body. This is a composite of what these ancient carvings looked like.

© Example of Neolithic petroglyph showing X-Man. Artwork by C. McHale

» According to *The Antiquities of the Jews,* Cain's name means "possession." It says, "Adam and Eve had two sons: the elder of them was named Cain; which name, when it is interpreted, signifies a possession" (Whiston, 1987). Eve said Cain was a possession because she had acquired this man from God. Possession is a fitting name for the Iceman because he is the most prized possession of the Bolzano museum and one of the greatest archaeological discoveries in history. The intense legal battle the Italians fought with the Austrians was not just for the prize ownership of a rare artifact. Possession of this body has generated tremendous income from tourism in that region. Otzi brings in millions of dollars a year. There are probably many Italians who would say, "We acquired this man from God."

» Early findings reported that the Iceman wore sheepskin. Cain wore sheepskin as well. In fact, Abel told him to take off the skin from his sheep when they were arguing, right before he murdered him. *The Ancient Book of Jasher* reads as follows:

> And Cain approached his brother Abel in anger, and he said unto him, What is there between me and thee, that thou comest to dwell and bring thy flock to feed in my land? And Abel answered his brother Cain and said unto him, What is there between me and thee, that thou shalt eat the flesh of my flock and clothe thyself with their wool? And now therefore, put off the wool of my sheep with which thou hast clothed thyself, and recompense me for their fruit and flesh which thou hast eaten, and when thou shalt have done this, I will then go from thy land as thou hast said? (Johnson, 2008)

» Traces of copper and arsenic were found in the Iceman's hair and under his fingernails, indicating that he was involved in metallurgy. Cain's family members are mentioned in the Bible to be metal forgers. Another meaning for Cain's name is "smith" or "metal forger."

» The Iceman was thought to be wealthy, a robber or a clan leader, because of his copper ax, which would have been of considerable value. Cain was wealthy because of the robberies he committed and was the clan leader of all his family. It is said that he filled his household with much wealth by rapine, violence, and robbery. He also became a great (powerful) leader of men into wicked courses.

» The Iceman's copper ax is almost identical to a Neolithic agricultural tool used for tilling the ground. Cain owned a Neolithic plowing tool he used to till the ground, and a plow head was used to kill Abel, according to one of the ancient books.

» The Iceman was thought to be a hunter because of the contents in his digestive system and the weapons he carried. Cain was a hunter and scavenger because he could not grow food himself after he killed Abel.

© *Cain the Hunter and Wanderer.* Artwork by O. Thomas

» The Iceman is thought to be a warrior because of the cut on his hand, the injuries on various parts of his body, and the blood of four others found on his coat and weapons, all of which indicated a physical confrontation. Cain and his progeny were said to be difficult to beat in battle and liked killing their victims slowly. He cared only about his own bodily pleasures even though it caused him to hurt others.

» There is a castle in the region from which archaeologists believe the Iceman came. It is named Castle Juval. Cain had a great-great-great-great-grandson named Jubal and was known to name places after his family members.

» The Iceman's possessions were left at the scene of the crime. Cain's great-great-great-grandson fled the murder scene in shock, probably carrying his son Tubal, whom he accidentally killed. There is no mention of him taking Cain's possessions.

» Someone removed the arrow shaft from the Iceman's body and possibly rolled him over. Lamech and Tubal went to see the game they had killed, and then examined the body and realized it was Cain. It is highly plausible that they rolled him over and pulled the arrow shaft out in an attempt to save him.

» In Italy, where the discovery took place, the day of the month is written first. That means it would read 19/9/1991, a mysterious date in itself. Is this number 1991991 symbolic for history repeating itself?

» Samuel 6:18 speaks of the stone of Abel, possibly a monument to Abel: " … even as far as the large stone of Abel on which they set the ark of the Lord, which stone remains to this day in the field of Joshua of Beth Shemesh." Some people believe the stone is still there to this day. If you travel to the mountain where the Iceman was found, you will also see a large stone that has been set up as a monument to Otzi. Both stones represent the memory of a man who was murdered by a stone.

There probably are more similarities yet to be discovered in the future. With all of the circumstantial evidence, it is almost as if God is saying, "Here is Cain. What are you going to do about it?" A curious play on words reveals the name Iceman actually has "me Cain" hidden within it. Do you believe Cain is hidden within the Iceman?

Of course the data will never be 100 percent conclusive; even so, we can judge the circumstantial evidence to a degree of certainty. Objectively analyzing all the data, we can suggest that this is either the greatest coincidence of all time or that this is the body of Cain. Speaking for myself, I find it beyond the scope of mere coincidence. I am persuaded by the volume and specific nature of the evidence that it is highly probable that this is none other than the infamous Cain. So there you have it, Watson! What do you make of all this? Has the jury come to a verdict?

Chapter 11

Are You Abel?

WHEN YOU LOOK at the face of the Iceman, are you staring at the first murderer, who has been made an example to all mankind? Was he preserved as a warning, a sign for us "not to go in the way of Cain"? When you look at the world around you, do you feel society is already headed the way of Cain? Let me ask you this: Can you imagine just one day on earth without any murders? It is almost inconceivable.

The way the scientific findings line up with the historical documents is profound. But beyond all the examinations, the evidence, and this mysterious mummy, what is the real message to be revealed here? What can we take from this old, cold, and lonely body to lead us closer to the truth, the way, and the life?

The real wisdom to be found in this book is that even

history, viewed through the lens of science, will still reveal God's invisible qualities: His eternal power, His divine nature, and most importantly His amazing love and grace. Can it be said the perfect form of wisdom is love? You see, God is a righteous judge and could have destroyed Cain in righteous judgment right after he killed Abel, but he loved him. God knew what was to come, but he still extended grace to Cain. God allowed him to live and have free will to choose to live in sin or turn away from it, just as he allows for every one of us. Cain would not turn away from his sin. Because he did not repent, God turned away from Cain and handed him over to his sin.

Cain's sin consumed him; it destroyed his life and became a generational curse. Imagine the pain it caused Adam and Eve, who loved both of their sons, to lose them both in one day! How do parents live with the pain of one child murdering the other? The very reason God does not want us to have sin in our lives is for our protection. He wants us to avoid the kind of deep, inflicting pain that can be passed down to other generations. God knows what the outcomes are when we cheat, murder, lie, commit adultery, become addicted to drugs and alcohol, disobey the law, and put other gods before him. Many people feel hatred and rebellion toward God and Christianity because they do not want to turn away from the sins they enjoy. Eventually, however, those sins will lead to death, and there is nothing I would fear more than dying without knowing the Lord. If you take the time to study about hell, you will understand what is really at stake.

The Bible is clear that God loves us so much, he sent his only Son to die for us so we someday could live with God for eternity. Before sin entered the world, God walked with man in the Garden of Eden. Adam, the first man God created, made a bad choice; he disobeyed God and caused a separation between God and man. Christ, who came in the form of both God and man, chose to obey God and became a bridge for mankind to cross over and be united with God once again. First Corinthians 15:45–49, in the New Living Translation, says the following:

> The Scriptures tell us, "The first man, Adam, became a living person." But the last Adam— that is, Christ—is a life-giving Spirit. What comes first is the natural body, then the spiritual body comes later. Adam, the first man, was made from the dust of the earth, while Christ, the second man, came from heaven. Earthly people are like the earthly man, and heavenly people are like the heavenly man. Just as we are now like the earthly man, we will someday be like the heavenly man.

Jesus, the second Adam, came to restore what the first Adam destroyed. I never understood the power of the cross until I learned about this verse in the Bible. God had to send a savior to reverse how Adam brought sin into the world. Adam's sin changed man from immortal to mortal beings by eating the fruit of the Tree of the Knowledge of Good and Evil. He directly disobeyed God, followed his own will, and handed mankind over to the bondage of sin. The first Adam broke the relationship between God and man in the garden with a tree. To restore man's relationship Jesus Christ came full circle to undo what Adam did. He knew He had to give himself over in the Garden of Gethsemane. Jesus was sweating blood and He considered His own will which would be to let this cup pass from Him. But He made the powerful statement in the garden, "Your will be done, not mine." He could have said one word and destroyed all of the soldiers; He could have called out legions of angels from heaven to fight for Him. He willingly gave himself as a living sacrifice knowing the horrific events about to take place. He was beaten and then nailed on a tree teaching us the true meaning of the knowledge of good and evil. There is nothing in the world as powerful as the cross. There is nothing that is so incredibly good but so inherently evil at the same time. What Christ did was so good that if you had the power to go back and save him from dying this death would you? On one hand we would like to say yes, we would prevent this terrible evil inflicted on an innocent man. But ultimately, we have to say no and agree Jesus had to die, and it was good what He did for us. It was so good and I am so thankful! Christ's atonement for our sins made it possible for us to live eternally with God once again. God sent Christ, who knew no sin, to become sin for us and He conquered sin and death. He paid for all of the sins of mankind, including Adam, by reversing what was done in the garden with a tree and leaving us with the bitter sweet taste of the fruit of the knowledge of good and evil. John 3:16, New King James Version, says, "For God so loved the world that He gave His only begotten Son, that whoever believes in Him should not perish but have everlasting life."

Contrary to popular belief, the Bible says there is only one way to heaven; it says no man will come to the Father except through the Son. And when we realize the magnitude of the sacrifice God made for us—although we are all still sinners, he gave his life for us because he loves us—a powerful transformation happens within our hearts. Even a heart that is broken, prideful, or waxing cold will melt in the presence of God's amazing love.

Once we experience the love of God, we want deeply to love one another and turn away from the sin that separates us from Him. First John 3:1 and 11–16, New Living Translation, is a part of Scripture that brings the entire message of this study into the right perspective:

> See how very much our Father loves us, for he calls us His children, and that is what we are! But the people who belong to this world don't recognize that we are God's children because they don't know Him …

> This is the message you have heard from the beginning: We should love one another. We must not be like Cain, who belonged to the evil one and killed his brother. And why did he kill him? Because Cain had been doing what was evil, and his brother had been doing what was righteous.

So don't be surprised, dear brothers and sisters, if the world hates you. If we love our Christian brothers and sisters, it proves that we have passed from death to life. But a person who has no love is still dead. Anyone who hates another brother or sister is really a murderer at heart. And you know that murderers don't have eternal life within them. We know what real love is because Jesus gave up His life for us.

My friend, whether you are the most faithful God-fearing man or a self-proclaimed atheist, my hope for you is that you will know you are loved by the One who created you. We cannot come to love one another unless we have the love of Christ in our hearts. And without love, we are full of hate. In fact, if you do not know the Lord, you could be feeling hatred or anger every time I mention God or the Bible in this book. Let that be a warning sign to you that something is wrong; you are being deceived.

You are precious to God and loved beyond what you could ever imagine. The Bible says, "Anyone who hates another brother or sister is really a murderer at heart." And without Christ's love, we are choosing to go the way of Cain—a path that leads to destruction. Cain committed the first murder because he was jealous of a righteous man. The legacy of Cain is this paradox: Cain hated his brother because he was good. The very essence of evil is found in this short statement in the Bible. The legacy of Abel is that he trusted God in everything.

His faith allowed him to endure the wickedness of his brother, saying to Cain, God will recompense you for any harm you do to me. These legacies have played out all through the history of mankind.

Let's take a look at the heart of Abel. Abel believed God was present in all of his actions. He wanted to please God and he wanted to know God. Abel said God would avenge his blood if Cain were to kill him. Maybe the reason for this study, more than 5,000 years later, is to see how the words of Abel became true. Hebrews 11:4 says, "It was by faith that Abel brought a more acceptable offering to God than Cain did. Abel's offering gave evidence that he was a righteous man, and God showed his approval of his gifts. Although Abel is long dead, he still speaks to us by his example of faith."

If we could hear Abel speak, I believe he would ask which brother we favor. Which legacy will we follow? We all are sinners, and every single one of us has walked in the way of Cain at some point in our lives. I can say that in the years of my youth, I was the prodigal son. I lived by the standards of the world and sought to please myself, but it did not take long to realize that I was empty. The sins I committed made me feel awful, and I wanted to repent, to turn away from my sin and be washed clean. The Bible says that anyone who is in Christ becomes a new creation, old things are washed away and all things become new. You can be made new!

So where are you today? Are you full of anger? Is your heart cold and jaded? Maybe you are a Christian but you feel hatred for another person. Is there someone you need to forgive in your life? Are you going the way of Cain or are you Abel? Are you able to receive the grace that has been extended to you? Are you able to express that same grace to others? Are you able to let go of the mistakes you made in the past and be made new?

Abel was a foreshadowing of Jesus because he was a good shepherd killed because he was righteous; he was obedient to God and found to be upright in his sight. The Bible says the blood of Christ speaks an even better word than that of Abel. Abel's blood cried out to God for justice, and Jesus' atoning blood cried out to God for mercy. Justice is what we deserve, but mercy is the gift God has given to us. John 3:17 says, For God sent not his Son into the world to condemn the world; but that the world through him might be saved. All you need to do is search for Him with all of your heart, repent of your sins, and ask Jesus to be your Savior. And that is what God wants for you, to accept the free gift of salvation and to get to know Him. The more you seek Him, the more you will find Him. And when you experience His love, you will want to have a heart like Abel's—warm, loving, and obedient to God.

The legacy of these two brothers will be remembered indefinitely. Many believe it was on the Day of Atonement when Cain and Abel made their offerings to God. The Iceman's body was discovered on September 19, 1991, on the Day of Atonement—a date with powerful spiritual significance. I think we can answer the question the rabbi asks on Yom Kippur, the very question God asked Cain: "Where is your brother?" Abel is certainly in heaven, brought up from Abraham's bosom by Christ himself. Remember, Abel's heart was in the right place, but Cain had an evil heart. He wanted to please himself rather than obey God. He could have turned from his sin and repented. God would have forgiven Cain even after killing Abel. Unfortunately, he refused to turn away from it, so God handed him over to his sin and it destroyed his life.

If we could ask Abel the exact same question—"Where is your brother?"—what would he say about his cold-blooded killer?

Cain's heart was selfish, deceitful, desperately wicked, and cold. In fact, some would say his heart was just as icy as a man frozen in a glacier for more than 5,000 years.

ADDENDUM:
ANCIENT HISTORICAL
RECORDS OF CAIN

It is important to be familiar with the ancient records of Cain. As a reference, I have added quotes from some of the most important, ancient, historical records I have found. There will be a brief description of each book before the quotations. I would like to encourage anyone reading this book to research these manuscripts further. Most of these books can be viewed online for free.

The Bible is the No.1- selling book in all of history. In fact, many people view the Bible as a history book. It has helped to shape world chronologies, and its records have been proven true and consistent in several archaeological and scientific findings. In addition to being a history book, the Bible is believed by approximately one-third of the world's population to be the divine Word of God. No matter how you view this book, it can be used as a reliable resource for historical records of real people.

The Holy Bible Genesis 4: 1-18 King James Version

"¹And Adam knew Eve his wife; and she conceived, and bare Cain, and said, I have gotten a man from the LORD. ²And she again bare his brother Abel. And Abel was a keeper of sheep, but Cain was a tiller of the ground. ³And in process of time it came to pass, that Cain brought of the fruit of the ground an offering unto the LORD. ⁴And Abel, he also brought of the firstlings of his flock and of the fat thereof. And the LORD had respect unto Abel and to his offering: ⁵But unto Cain and to his offering he had not respect. And Cain was very wroth, and his countenance fell. ⁶And the LORD said unto Cain, Why art thou wroth? and why is thy countenance fallen? ⁷If thou doest well, shalt thou not be accepted? and if thou doest not well, sin lieth at the door. And unto thee shall be his desire, and thou shalt rule over him."

Verse 3 states: "In the process of time Cain brought an offering." In Hebrew the process of time is the word "Qets," which is to say "at the end of time." This is almost certainly a reference to the Jubilee year. English Bible translators either did not understand or had difficulty with the concept of the Jubilee cycle. In their translations, they would use obscure phrases such as, "In the course of those many years" or "when the appointed time had come." Even in the New Testament we see a Jubilee referenced as, "In the fullness of time." These references correspond to the occurrence of the 49-year Jubilee cycle culminating in a year of Jubilee. These Jubilee references are the only method by which we can establish an accurate timeline. Adam would have been 98 years old, Abel would have been 22 years old, and Cain would have been 29 years old when he killed Abel.

In verse 7, we see God's instruction to Cain to master his evil countenance and not fall under the control of sin. Even though God spoke directly to Cain, he willfully rebelled against God.

"[8]And Cain talked with Abel his brother: and it came to pass, when they were in the field, that Cain rose up against Abel his brother, and slew him. [9]And the LORD said unto Cain, Where is Abel thy brother? And he said, I know not: Am I my brother's keeper? [10]And he said, What hast thou done? The voice of thy brother's blood crieth unto me from the ground."

Abel's voice crying to God is the first testimony of life after death.

"[11]And now art thou cursed from the earth, which hath opened her mouth to receive thy brother's blood from thy hand; [12]When thou tillest the ground, it shall not henceforth yield unto thee her strength; a fugitive and a vagabond shalt thou be in the earth."

Cain is cursed from the earth that has become Abel's resting place. In contrast to Abel returning to the earth, dust to dust,

Cain is prohibited from returning to the earth, both in life for sustenance, and in death for a resting place.

"[13]And Cain said unto the LORD, My punishment is greater than I can bear. [14]Behold, thou hast driven me out this day from the face of the earth; and from thy face shall I be hid; and I shall be a fugitive and a vagabond in the earth; and it shall come to pass, that every one that findeth me shall slay me. [15]And the LORD said unto him, therefore whosoever slayeth Cain, vengeance shall be taken on him sevenfold. And the LORD set a mark upon Cain, lest any finding him should kill him. [16]And Cain went out from the presence of the LORD, and dwelt in the land of Nod, on the east of Eden [17]And Cain knew his wife; and she conceived, and bare Enoch: and he builded a city, and called the name of the city, after the name of his son, Enoch. [18]And unto Enoch was born Irad: and Irad begat Mehujael: and Mehujael begat Methusael: and Methusael begat Lamech. [19]And Lamech took unto him two wives: the name of the one was Adah, and the name of the other Zillah. [20]And Adah bare Jabal: he was the father of such as dwell in tents, and of such as have cattle. [21]And his brother's name was Jubal: he was the father of all such as handle the harp and organ. [22]And Zillah, she also bare Tubalcain, an instructer of every artificer in brass and iron: and the sister of Tubalcain was Naamah. [23]And Lamech said unto his wives, Adah and Zillah, Hear my voice; ye wives of Lamech, hearken unto my speech: for I have slain a man to my wounding, and a young man to my hurt. [24]If Cain shall be avenged sevenfold, truly Lamech seventy and sevenfold."

Verses 23 and 24 relate Lamech's confession to the slaying of two people—a man and a young man. These murders result in the curse of Cain being transferred and compounded onto Lamech 77-fold. This connection to the curse of Cain amounts to a confession from Lamech to the murder of Cain. The Ancient Book of Jasher has more information on the death of Cain.

The Ancient Book of Jasher was considered a lost book throughout many years in history. There have been at least two false documents printed claiming to be the Ancient Book of Jasher that were fradulant, which has created much speculation about the book in general. The original Hebrew version was printed first in Naples in 1552 and later in Venice in 1625. The printer, Joseph Samuel, said the work was copied from an ancient manuscript. Many scholars consider this to be the authentic book, referenced in the Old Testament because the preface traces the original source of the book and the manuscript closely matches the Biblical history up until the time of Jacob. The preface states the original source book came out of a hidden library in the ruins of Jerusalem in 70 A.D. A Roman officer is credited with saving the book and bringing it back to his home in Spain. The manuscript was later bought by a Jewish college in Cordova, Spain, where scholars apparently had preserved the book until its printings.

The Ancient Book of Jasher is quoted at least twice in the Bible; Joshua 10:13 states: "Is not this written in the Book of Jasher?" This refers to a passage found in Jasher 88:64. Additionally, 2

Samuel 1:18 states: "Behold it is written in the Book of Jasher." This refers to a passage found in Jasher 56:9. The name Jasher is not the author's name; it means the faithful witness.

Ancient Book of Jasher 1: 12–35

"And it was at the expiration of a few years, that they brought an approximating offering to the Lord, and Cain brought from the fruit of the ground, and Abel brought from the firstlings of his flock from the fat thereof, and God turned and inclined to Abel and his offering, and a fire came down from the Lord from heaven and consumed it. And unto Cain and his offering the Lord did not turn, and he did not incline to it, for he had brought from the inferior fruit of the ground before the Lord, and Cain was jealous against his brother Abel on account of this, and he sought a pretext to slay him. And in some time after, Cain and Abel his brother, went one day into the field to do their work; and they were both in the field, Cain tilling and ploughing his ground, and Abel feeding his flock; and the flock passed that part which Cain had ploughed in the ground, and it sorely grieved Cain on this account. And Cain approached his brother Abel in anger, and he said unto him, What is there between me and thee, that thou comest to dwell and bring thy flock to feed in my land? And Abel answered his brother Cain and said unto him, What is there between me and thee, that thou shalt eat the flesh of my flock and clothe thyself with their wool? And now therefore, put off the wool of my sheep with which thou hast clothed thyself, and recompense me for their fruit and flesh which thou hast eaten, and when thou shalt have done this, I will then go from thy land as thou hast said? And Cain said to his brother Abel, Surely if I slay thee this day, who will require thy blood from me? And Abel answered Cain, saying, Surely God who has made us in the earth, he will avenge my cause, and he will require my blood from thee shouldst thou slay me, for the Lord is the judge and arbiter, and it is he who will requite man according to his evil, and the wicked man according to the wickedness that he may do upon earth. And now, if thou shouldst slay me here, surely God knoweth thy secret views, and will judge thee for the evil which thou didst declare to do unto me this day. And when Cain heard the words which Abel his brother had spoken, behold the anger of Cain was kindled against his brother Abel for declaring this thing. And Cain hastened and rose up, and took the iron part of his ploughing instrument, with which he suddenly smote his brother and he slew him, and Cain spilt the blood of his brother Abel upon the earth, and the blood of Abel streamed upon the earth before the flock" (Johnson, 2008).

The tip, or the metal part, of Cain's hand plough is the infamous weapon used for the world's first murder.

"And after this Cain repented having slain his brother, and he was sadly grieved, and he wept over him and it vexed him exceedingly. And Cain rose up and dug a hole in the field, wherein he put his brother's body, and he turned the dust over it. And the Lord knew what Cain had done to his brother, and the Lord appeared to Cain and said unto him, Where is Abel thy brother that was with thee? And Cain dissembled, and said, I do not know, am I my brother's keeper? And the Lord said unto him, What hast thou done? The voice of thy brother's blood crieth unto me from the ground where thou hast slain him. For thou hast slain thy brother and hast dissembled before me, and didst imagine in thy heart that I saw thee not, nor knew all thy actions. But thou didst this thing and didst slay thy brother for naught and because he spoke rightly to thee, and now, therefore, cursed be thou from the ground which opened its mouth to receive thy brother's blood from thy hand, and wherein thou didst bury him. And it shall be when thou shalt till it, it shall no more give thee its strength as in the beginning, for thorns and thistles shall the ground produce, and thou shalt be moving and wandering in the earth until the day of thy death. And at that time Cain went out from the presence of the Lord, from the place where he was, and he went moving and wandering in the land toward the east of Eden, he and all belonging to him. And Cain knew his wife in those days, and she conceived and bare a son, and he called his name Enoch, saying, In that time the Lord began to give him rest and quiet in the earth. And at that time Cain also began to build a city: and he built the city and he called the name of the city Enoch, according to the name of his son; for in those days the Lord had given him rest upon the earth, and he did not move about and wander as in the beginning" (Johnson, 2008).

Take note the Ancient Book of Jasher's account specifically

says Cain would be cursed from the ground in which Abel was buried: "cursed be thou from the ground which opened its mouth to receive thy brother's blood from thy hand, and wherein thou didst bury him."

Ancient Book of Jasher 2: 26-36

"And Lamech was old and advanced in years, and his eyes were dim that he could not see, and Tubal Cain, his son, was leading him and it was one day that Lamech went into the field and Tubal Cain his son was with him, and whilst they were walking in the field, Cain the son of Adam advanced towards them; for Lamech was very old and could not see much, and Tubal Cain his son was very young.

"And Tubal Cain told his father to draw his bow, and with the arrows he smote Cain, who was yet far off, and he slew him, for he appeared to them to be an animal. And the arrows entered Cain's body although he was distant from them, and he fell to the ground and died.

"And the Lord requited Cain's evil according to his wickedness, which he had done to his brother Abel, according to the word of the Lord which he had spoken. And it came to pass when Cain had died, that Lamech and Tubal went to see the animal which they had slain, and they saw, and behold Cain their grandfather was fallen dead upon the earth. And Lamech was very much grieved at having done this, and in clapping his hands together he struck his son and caused his death.

"And the wives of Lamech heard what Lamech had done, and they sought to kill him. And the wives of Lamech hated him from that day, because he slew Cain and Tubal Cain, and the wives of Lamech separated from him, and would not hearken to him in those days.

"And Lamech came to his wives, and he pressed them to listen to him about this matter. And he said to his wives Adah and Zillah, Hear my voice O wives of Lamech, attend to my words, for now you have imagined and said that I slew a man with my wounds, and a child with my stripes for their having done no violence, but surely know that I am old and grey-headed, and that my eyes are heavy through age, and I did this thing unknowingly.

"And the wives of Lamech listened to him in this matter, and they returned to him with the advice of their father Adam, but they bore no children to him from that time, knowing that God's anger was increasing in those days against the sons of men, to destroy them with the waters of the flood for their evil doings" (Johnson, 2008).

The Antiquities of the Jews by Flavius Josephus is a first-century history book. Josephus was a Jewish priest who was captured by the Romans during the Judean war of 70 A.D. He actually witnessed the temple being destroyed and the decimation of his people. He found favor with Emperor Titus, who allowed him to save many priests and ancient books from the Temple at

Jerusalem. The Antiquities of the Jews was written around 94 A.D. using the records he saved.

Flavius Josephus Antiquities of the Jews Book One, Chapter 2

"CONCERNING THE POSTERITY OF ADAM, AND THE TEN GENERATIONS FROM HIM TO THE DELUGE,

1. ADAM and Eve had two sons: the elder of them was named Cain; which name, when it is interpreted, signifies a possession. The younger was Abel, which signifies sorrow. They had also daughters. Now, the two brethren were pleased with different courses of life, for Abel, the younger, was a lover of righteousness, and, believing that God was present at all his actions, he excelled in virtue; and his employment was that of a shepherd. But Cain was not only very wicked in other respects, but was wholly intent upon getting; and he first contrived to plough the ground. He slew his brother on the occasion following : They had resolved to sacrifice to God. Now Cain brought the fruits of the earth, and of his husbandry; but Abel brought milk, and the firstfruits of his flocks: but God was more delighted with the latter oblation, when he was honored with what grew naturally of its own accord, than he was with what was the invention of a covetous man, and gotten by forcing the ground; whence it was that Cain was very angry that Abel was preferred by God before him; and he slew his brother, and hid his dead body, thinking to escape discovery. But God, knowing what had been done, came to Cain, and asked him what was become of his brother,

because he had not seen him of many days; whereas he used to observe them conversing together at other times. But Cain was in doubt with himself, and knew not what answer to give to God. At first he said that he was himself at a loss about his brother's disappearing; but when he was provoked by God, who pressed him vehemently, as resolving to know what the matter was, he replied, he was not his brother's guardian or keeper, nor was he an observer of what he did. But, in return, God convicted Cain, as having been the murderer of his brother; and said, 'I wonder at thee, that thou knowest not what is become of a man whom thou thyself hast destroyed.' God therefore did not inflict the punishment [of death] upon him, on account of his offering sacrifice, and thereby making supplication to him not to be extreme in his wrath to him; but he made him accursed, and threatened his posterity in the seventh generation. He also cast him, together with his wife, out of that land. And when he was afraid that in wandering about he should fall among Wild beasts, and by that means perish, God bid him not to entertain such a melancholy suspicion, and to go over all the earth without fear of what mischief he might suffer from wild beasts; and setting a mark upon him, that he might be known, he commanded him to depart.

2. And when Cain had traveled over many countries, he, with his wife, built a city, named Nod, which is a place so called, and there he settled his abode; where also he had children" (Whiston,1987).

Here we have evidence Cain traveled far distances. He settled in a location considered to be another country and at least some distance from the land now called Israel.

"However, he did not accept of his punishment, in order to amendment, but to increase his wickedness; for he only aimed to procure everything that was for his own bodily pleasure, though it obliged him to be injurious to his neighbors. He augmented his household substance with much wealth, by rapine and violence; he excited his acquaintance to procure pleasures and spoils by robbery, and became a great leader of men into wicked courses. He also introduced a change in that way of simplicity wherein men lived before; and was the author of measures and weights. And whereas they lived innocently and generously while they knew nothing of such arts, he changed the world into cunning craftiness. He first of all set boundaries about lands; he built a city, and fortified it with walls, and he compelled his family to come together to it; and called that city Enoch, after the name of his eldest son Enoch. Now Jared was the son of Enoch; whose son was Malaliel; whose son was Mathusela; whose son was Lamech; who had seventy-seven children by two wives, Silla and Ada. Of those children by Ada, one was Jabal; he erected tents, and loved the life of a shepherd. But Jubal, who was born of the same mother with him, exercised himself in music; and invented the psaltery and the harp. But Tubal, one of his children by the other wife, exceeded all men in strength, and was very expert and famous in martial performances. He procured what tended to the pleasures of the body by that method; and first of all invented the art of making brass. Lamech was also the father of a daughter, whose name was Naamah; and because he was so skillful in matters of divine revelation, that he knew he was to be punished for Cain's murder of his brother, he made that known to his wives. Nay, even while Adam was alive, it came to pass that the posterity of Cain became exceeding wicked, every one successively dying one after another more wicked than the former. They were intolerable in war, and vehement in robberies; and if any one were slow to murder people, yet was he bold in his profligate behavior, in acting unjustly, and doing injuries for gain" (Whiston,1987).

The Book of Jubilees is an ancient Hebrew history that parallels the Books of Genesis and Exodus (Vermes, 2004). It must have been regarded highly by the Orthodox Jews because portions of 15 different copies were found in the Dead Sea Scrolls, more than any other book apart from the Biblical texts. This book also was reguarded highly by the early church fathers and still is part of the Ethoptic Bible.

The Book of Jubilees Chapter 4: 1-5

"And in the third week in the second jubilee she gave birth to Cain, and in the fourth jubilee she gave birth to Abel, and in the fifth jubilee she gave birth to her daughter Âwân. And in the first year of the third jubilee (this is the Year of Jubilee, the 50th year), Cain killed Abel because God accepted the sacrifice of Abel, and did not accept the offering of Cain. And he killed him in the field, and his blood cried from the ground to heaven, complaining because he had killed him. The Lord blamed Cain, because he killed Abel, and He made him a fugitive on the earth because of the blood of his brother, and He cursed him on the earth. Because of this it is written on the heavenly tablets, 'Cursed is he who kills his neighbor treacherously, and let all who have seen and heard say, 'So be it,' and the man who has seen and not reported it, let him be accursed as the one committing it." (Lumpkin, 2006).

The Book of Jubilees Chapter 4: 9-10

"And Cain took Awan his sister to be his wife and she gave birth to Enoch at the close of the fourth jubilee. In the first year of the first week of the fifth jubilee, houses were built on earth, and Cain built a city, and called its name after the name of his son Enoch" (Lumpkin, 2006).

BIBLIOGRAPHY

Acs P., Wilhalm, T., & Oeggl, K. (2005). Remains of grasses found with the Neolithic Iceman "Otzi." Veget Hist Archaeobot. Vol. 14, 198-206.

Aquaron, M. (2005, July). Ötzi, witness and messenger of our past. Hominides.com. Retrieved February 9, 2012, from http://translate.google.com/translate?hl=en&prev=/sear ch%3Fq%3DEpulopiscium%252&rurl=translate.google. com&sl=fr&u=http://www.hominides.com/html/ ancetres/otzi2.php

Aquaron, M. (2008). Latest news from Ötzi, the Iceman. Hominides.com. Retrieved February 9, 2012, from http://translate.googleusercontent.com/ translate_c?hl=en&prev=/search%3Fq%3DEpulopiscium %2Bfishelsoni,%2Botzi%26hl%3Den%26safe%3Doff%2 6biw%3D1280%26bih%3D617%26prmd%3Dimvns&rur

l=translate.google.com&sl=fr&twu=1&u=http://www.
hominides.com/html/ancetres/otzi3.php&usg=ALkJrhgJ
mKGa1YrFDy1vhzZoQzDg1AkV0w

ALPHABET, HEBREW. (2012). Jewish Virtual Library a division of the American-Israeli Cooperative Enterprise. Retrieved February 12, 2012, from http://www.jewishvirtuallibrary. org/jsource/judaica/ejud_0002_0001_0_00876.html

Ancient Hebrew Research Center (1999). Plowing Through History, From Aleph to Tav. Ancient Hebrew Research Center. Retrieved March 2, 2012, from http://www. ancient-hebrew.org/3_waw.html

Ancient Hebrew Research Center (1999). Plowing Through History, From Aleph to Tav. Ancient Hebrew Research Center. Retrieved March 2, 2012, from http://www. ancient-hebrew.org/3 lam.html

Bahn, P. G. (2005). OTZI THE ICEMAN. Dig, 7(4), 14.

Bahn, P. G. (2009). WHY LINES AND CROSSES? Dig, 11(6), 8.

BBC Horizon. (2002). "Death of the Iceman" [TV]. England.

Benhamou, G., & Sabroux, J. (2006). In La Malediction D'Otzi / The Curse of Otzi. (1st ed.). Paris, France: Plon.

Biblos.com (n.d.). Meaning of the Hebrew word "Oth"search. Concordances.org. Retrieved February 27, 2012, from http://concordances.org/hebrew/2053.htm

Biblos.com (n.d.) Meaning of the Name "Cain" search. Retrieved March 5, 2012, from http://topicalbible.org/c/cain.htm

Death renews iceman "curse" claim. (2005, November 5). BBC News. Retrieved June 7, 2009, from http://news.bbc.co.uk/2/hi/europe/4409512.stm

Ermini, L., Olivieri, C., Rizzi, E., Corti, G., Bonnal, R., Soares, P.,...Rollo, F. (2008). Complete Mitochondrial Genome Sequence of the Tyrolean Iceman. Current Biology, 18, 1687-1693.

Fitzpatrick, A. (2011, February 17). The Amesbury Archer: The King of Stonehenge? BBC History. Retrieved November 10, 2011, from http://www.bbc.co.uk/history/ancient/archaeology/king_stonehenge_01.shtml

Fowler, B. (2000). Iceman: Uncovering the Life and Times of a Prehistoric Man Found in an Alpine Glacier. (1st ed.). New York, New York/ United States: Random House.

Gaivin, K. (2009). The Iceman cometh. Dermatology Times, 30(4), 18.

Goldberg, R. (Producer), & Quilici, B. (Director). (2003) "Iceman: Hunt for a Killer" [TV]. United States.

Google Earth 6.2 [Software]: Google Inc. (2012). [Search Stele di Otzi, to the Gulf of Aqaba in the Red Sea] Available from http://www.google.com/intl/en/earth/index.html

Hall, S. S. (2007, July). Iceman Mystery. National Geographic. Retrieved September 13, 2011, from http://ngm. nationalgeographic.com/print/2007/07/iceman/hall-text

Haines, T., & McMaster, J. (Producers). (1998, November 24). A BBC/Horizon NOVA/WGBH Co-production. Transcripts:"Ice Mummies: Return of the Iceman". NOVA. Retrieved August 20, 2011, from http://www.pbs.org/wgbh/nova/transcripts/2518iceman.html

Howorth, H. H. (1887). Evidence of sudden and wide-spread Flood. In The Mammoth and the Flood. (1st ed.). (pp. 209-212). London, England: Sampson Low, Marston, Searle, & Rivington.

Iceman "probably killed by own people." (2002, November 14). BBC News World Edition. Retrieved May 5, 2009, from http://news.bbc.co.uk/2/hi/uk_news/england/2468905.stm

Johnson, K. (2008). Ancient Book Of Jasher. (1st ed.). Lexington, Kentucky: Biblefacts Ministries.

Kabbalah Centre International, Inc. (2004). The Zohar, Vol 1. Beresheet A, Section 48:458.

Keller, A.,Graefen, A., Ball, M., Matzas, M., Boisguerin, V., Maixner, F., Leidinger, P., Backes, C., Khairat, R., Forster, M., Stade, B., Franke, A., Mayer, J., Spangler, J., McLaughlin, S., Shah, M., Lee, C., Harkins, T., Sartori, A., Moreno-Estrada, A., Henn, B., Sikora, M., Semino, O., Chiaroni, J., Rootsi, S., Myres, N., Cabrera, V., Underhill, P., Bustamante, C., Vigl, E., Samadelli, M., Cipollini, G., Haas, J., Katus, H., O'Connor, B., Carlson, M., Meder, B., Blin, N., Meese, E., Pusch, C., & Zinc, A. (2012). New insights into the Tyrolean Iceman's origin and phenotype as inferred by whole-genome sequencing. Nature Communications, 3(698).

Kutschera, W. (n.d.). 4.4 Radiocarbon dating of the Iceman Otzi with accelerator mass spectrometry. Institute of Isotope Research and Nuclear Physics University of Vienna, 1-9.

Lorey, F. (1994). Tree Rings and Biblical Chronology. Institute for Creation Research. Retrieved March 6, 2012, from http://www.icr.org/article/tree-rings-biblical-chronology/

Loy, T. (1998). Blood on the axe. New Scientist Archive, 159(2151), 40.

Lumpkin, J. (2006). The Book of Jubilees. (1st ed.). Blountsville, Alabama: Fifth Estate.

Mazza, C. (2008). The past examined by a modern eye, a prehistoric case? Child's Nervous System, 24(10), 1083.

Murphy Jr, W. A., Nedden, D. Z., Gostner, P., Knapp, R., Recheis, W., & Seidler, H. (2003). The Iceman: Discovery and Imaging. Radiology, 226, 614-629. Retrieved from http://radiology.rsna.org/content/226/3/614.full

Mystery demise of Oetzi iceman is finally solved. (2001). Geographical (Campion Interactive Publishing), 73(10), 10.

Nerlich, A., Peschel, O., & Egarter-Vigl, E. (2009). New evidence for Ötzi's final trauma. Intensive Care Medicine, 35(6).

Nerlich, A., Bachmeier, B., Zink, A., Thalhammer, S., & Egarter-Vigl, E. (2003). Otzi had a wound on his right hand. Lancet, 362(9380), 334.

Nyland, A. (2010). Enoch's Second Journey. In Complete Books of Enoch: 1 Enoch (First Book of Enoch), 2 Enoch (Secrets of Enoch), 3 Enoch (Hebrew Book of Enoch. (1st ed.). (p. 48). Mermaid Beach, Qld., Australia: Smith and Stirling Publishers.

Oeggl, K., Kofler, W., Schmidl, A., Dickson, J. H., Egarter-Vigl, E., & Gaber, O. (2007). The reconstruction of the last itinerary of "Ötzi," the Neolithic Iceman, by pollen analyses from sequentially sampled gut extracts. Quaternary Science Reviews, 26, 853-861.

Pabst, M. A., Letofsky-Papst, I., Bock, E., Moser, M., Dorfer, L., Egarter-Vigl, E., & Hofer, F. (2009). The tattoos of the Tyrolean Iceman: a light microscopical, ultrastructural and element analytical study. Journal of Archaeological Science, 36(10).

Pain, S. (2001, July 26). Arrow points to foul play in ancient iceman's death. NewScientist. Retrieved February 9, 2012, from http://www.newscientist.com/article/dn1080

Petrie, W. F. (1906). Chapter 9, The Lesser and Foreign Monuments. In Researches in Sinai. (pp. 130-132). London, England: General Books LLC, J. Murray.

Ravilious, K. (2008, December 4). Wounded Iceman Made Epic Final Journey, Moss Shows. National Geographic News. Retrieved April 25, 2009, from http://news.nationalgeographic.com/news/2008/12/081204-iceman-moss.html

Ridge, K. K. (2003). Who Killed the Iceman? Know Your World Extra, 37(3), 12.

Rollo, F. U. (2002). Ötzi's last meals: DNA analysis of the intestinal content of the Neolithic glacier mummy from the Alps. PNAS, 99.

Rollo, F. U., Ermini, L., Luciani, S., Marota, I., Olivieri, C., & Luiselli, D. (2006). Fine characterization of the Iceman's mtDNA Haplogroup. American Journal of Physical Anthropology, 130.

Rollo, F., Luciani, S., Marota, I., Olivieri, C., & Ermini, L. (2007). Persistence and decay of the intestinal microbiota's DNA in glacier mummies from the Alps. Journal of Archaeological Science, 34(8), 1294-1305.

Root-Bernstein, R. S. (1995, September 1). Darwin's Rib. Discover Magazine. Retrieved August 2011, from http://discovermagazine.com/1995/sep/darwinsrib561

Ruff, C. B., Holt, B.M., Sládek, V., Berner, M., Murphy Jr, W., Nedden, D., Seidler, H., Recheis, W. (2006). Body size, body proportions, and mobility in the Tyrolean "Iceman." Journal of Human Evolution. 51(1).

South Tyrol Museum of Archaeology. (2011). Retrieved November 14, 2011, from http://www.iceman.it/en/oetzi-intact

South Tyrol Museum of Archaeology. (2011). Retrieved November 14, 2011, http://www.iceman.it/en/node/260

South Tyrol Museum of Archaeology. (2011). Retrieved July 7, 2011, http://www.iceman.it/en/node/243

Spindler, K. (1996). The Man In The Ice. (1st ed.). Toronto, Canada: Doubleday Canada Limited.

Tyrolean Iceman is the end of his line. (2008, October 31). Cordis News. Retrieved November 11, 2011, from http://cordis.europa.eu/fetch?CALLER=EN_ NEWS&ACTION=D&RCN=30050

Ussher, J. (1658). The First Age of the World. In Ussher's Annals of the World. (1st ed.). (p. 13). London, England: E. Tyler.

Vermes, G. (2004). The Complete Dead Sea Scrolls in English. (8th ed.). London, England: Pelican Group.

Viegas, J. (2009, July 17). Oetzi Iceman's Tattoos Came from Fireplace. Discovery News. Retrieved February 9, 2012, from http://dsc.discovery.com/news/2009/07/17/iceman-tattoos.html

Whiston, W. (1987). The Works of Josephus. (14th ed.). Peabody, Maine: Hendrickson Publishers Inc.

Willard, L. (1960). Radiocarbon dating. American Journal of Science. 593-610.

© *Cain in the Land of Nod*. Artwork by O. Thomas

Special thanks to Jerry Porter, our developing editor.

Special thanks to "JP," our pictographic model.